HUNGERS OF THE HEART

Spirituality and Religion for the 21st Century

HUNGERS OF THE HEART

Spirituality and Religion for the 21st Century

Richard G. Watts

This book honors the life and thought of

Carl L. Esenwein

1934 – 2006

Photo Courtesy of Willem G.J. Knibbe

"Life as we know it is fragmentary. So is truth as we know it. Let us take what truth we can be sure of and use it boldly, for if we don't struggle to believe too much, at least we can be sure of what we cannot escape believing."

TABLE OF CONTENTS

Introduction

If you're at all like me, when you open up a new book, you browse through the first few pages to see whether it deals with questions that matter to you, whether it might make any difference in the way you live your life—in short, whether it's worth your time.

Here are a few questions that might help you decide.

- *Do you tend to think of yourself as "spiritual" rather than "religious?"*
- *Do you find yourself "turned off" by organized religion?*
- *Are you skeptical of the faith claims you grew up with?*
- *Do you doubt claims—whether by Pope, Bible or TV evangelist—to have "the" truth?*
- *Do you think science is a more reliable guide than Genesis or Revelation to where we came from and where we're going?*

If you answered "Yes" to any of these questions, this may be a book for you.

This book is about the "hungers of the heart" that all human beings long to satisfy. We are hungry to find a personal reason for being here, a purpose worth living for. We are hungry to shed our loneliness, to have honest relationships with other people. We are hungry for a society that is more peaceable and fair. And we are hungry to feel "at home" in the cosmos we so briefly inhabit; many call that a hunger to know God.

But as soon as we use that word, "God," we run into trouble, because it means so many different things to different people. Most of us grew up with some connection to Christianity; even if not part of a church, we inhabit a cultural world formed by the church and its language. The problem is that much of that inherited worldview doesn't feed our hungers any more. You've probably spotted bumper stickers like this one:

God said it

I believe it

That settles it—

but for many of us it's not settled at all. We think of the "good life" not as a cosmic truth that has been revealed from on high but as an unfolding human response to our particular historical moment. And we are comfortable with ambiguity, with partial answers to life's big questions. Now-familiar words of the poet Rainer Maria Rilke speak to us: "Be patient toward all that is unsolved in your heart and try to love the questions themselves…. Live the questions now. Perhaps you will then gradually, without noticing it, live along some distant day into the answer." We are people of search, not certainty.

On the other hand, we've got a hunch that the great world religions can't just be written off as ancient superstition. A rash of books by the "new atheists" with titles like *The God Delusion* and *God Is Not Great* have scoured the centuries for every horrible example of religious bigotry, ignorance and violence they could find, and damned the whole enterprise. They're right to be appalled, but not right to tar all religion with the brush of the worst abuses. My guess is that you don't picture a Jesus who would bash gays, cover up for priestly pedophiles, or beat the drums for holy war. So in these pages, while not whitewashing the dark side of religion, we'll be looking at its more authentic core, its open, compassionate, healing side. At its best, religion has always been a response to those "hungers of the heart." True, other generations used words that sound strange to us—words like "salvation," "grace," "resurrection," even "God." But if we can uncover the real human experience behind them, we might find that we have more in common with earlier generations than we realized—and even find *our own words* for our shared spiritual experience.

Many believe that it's *wrong* to re-think inherited religious views. A recent video series called "Living the Questions" posed the issue:

> "In virtually every field of human endeavor, new discoveries are praised. Not so with religion. In no area of life other than religion is the denial of progress held up as a virtue. Somehow, the way it was done in days-gone-by holds a mysterious authority over people. Twenty-first century believers faithfully recite creeds reflecting arcane fourth century questions with little thought given to the political and theological terrain that spawned the creeds in the first place."

In this book, I invite you to dare to re-imagine religion, to exercise your critical wits as a twenty-first century person, bringing along to the conversation whatever you may know of galaxies and DNA, bonobos and neurobiology, Buddhism and atheism. It's no virtue to leave our brains outside the door when we enter the sanctuary.

I need to say a word about two terms I've already used: "spiritual" and "religious." For many people in our day, "spiritual" is a good word, and "religious" is a bad word. Words are known by the company they keep: *spiritual* in our day keeps company with words like *personal, search, authentic,* and *experience,* while *religious* hangs out with *dogmatic, authoritarian,* and *exclusive.* As I see it, both words really refer to a common reality: the human quest to understand oneself in the whole cosmic context. You might think of it this way: *spirituality is personal religion, and religion is social spirituality.* Each can conjure up both positive and negative images: people who call themselves *spiritual* may be arrogant, while those who prefer *religious* may be open-minded, and *vice versa.* I'll use both words as referring to the same human impulse to find our place in the overall scheme of things; if one of those words turns you off, feel free to substitute the other.

This book is an unusual collaboration. Carl Esenwein, to whom it is dedicated, was a friend of mine who died four years ago, after a long struggle with cancer. In the early sixties, with his wife and three children, he left the business world, pulled up stakes and went to seminary in order to become a Unitarian minister. (You can learn more about him in the *Afterword.*) I came to know him late in his life, and greatly valued his wisdom, as I did his friendship. Over breakfast at IHOP (to which Carl brought home-brewed coffee, because IHOP's wasn't strong enough!) we often talked over the sorts of questions dealt with in these pages, and found that we saw things eye-to-eye. When his doctors told him that there was nothing more they could do, and it was clear that he hadn't many more months to live, I asked Carl if he would bequeath his writings to me, so that I might share his thinking with others. I've been living with those files for several years now, and they have become the basis of this book. Carl, of course, would not have spoken today exactly as he did three or four decades ago and, as he once said to me as he reflected on his ministry, "I would have told more stories." So I have freely updated many of his references, "told more stories," and added new material (e.g. the chapter "Beyond a Stingy God").

Nonetheless, the book's major themes are Carl's, and those of you who knew him as minister and teacher will surely hear his voice in these pages. While I accept responsibility for the final form of the book, I'm confident that the words I have added fit snugly into his way of looking at the place of spirituality in our life and world. I am grateful to be able to offer these pages as our shared reflection.

Carl never pretended to have all the answers to life's quandaries. "Life as we know it," he said, "is fragmentary. So is truth as we know it. Let us take what truth we can be sure of and use it boldly, for if we don't struggle to believe too much, at least we can be sure of what we cannot escape believing."

In that spirit, I invite you to think along with us about the hungers of our hearts, not claiming to understand too much, but being open to what we can't avoid affirming.

Dick Watts

Chapter 1

Our Hunger to Be "At Home" in the Cosmos

One of the deep hungers of the human heart is to feel "at home" and welcome in the universe we so briefly inhabit. As one seeker recently put it, "As my forties lengthened, I inexplicably became ravenous for wisdom and meaning. ...We are adrift in galaxies of mere information, distracted by the relentless drone of the e-hive, and I ached for the oxygen of understanding, which is always in short supply. ...Simply put, something deep and beyond articulation moved in my soul." Many call that "something deep and beyond articulation" a hunger for God, as in the oft-remembered prayer of the fifth century Christian saint, Augustine: "Our hearts are always restless, until they rest in You."

But, of course, "God" is simply a three-letter word, and everything depends upon what a person means by it. As we listen to God-talk in our culture, we hear a bewildering variety of contexts for that small word. Consider a few examples:

- A major league baseball player, his batting average mired around .200, says that he'll hit his 30 homers and drive in 100 runs when the "Good Man above [who] controls everything" lets him do so.

- An NFL starter cancels his retirement in order to play one more season because "God persuaded me to come back, and I always listen to what God says."

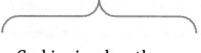

- A newspaper article on rising gasoline prices notes several contributing factors: war, the habits of drivers, and "an act of God," which turns out to be "an unusually cold winter."

God is simply a three-letter word, and everything depends upon what a person means by it.

- A 28-year-old woman, who didn't like to use condoms, awaiting test results after intimacy with her HIV-positive lover, opines that "if God is going to take me, He's going to take me anyway."

- A Member of Congress is overheard by *The Wall Street Journal* after Hurricane Katrina had devastated New Orleans:

"We finally cleaned up public housing in New Orleans. We couldn't do it, but God did."

- And others interpreted Katrina as God's judgment wreaked upon the city because of the "sin of shedding blood through abortion" or "25,000 homosexuals [who] were going to be celebrating sin in the streets."

If we stitch all these conversation scraps together, what kind of God do we get? Apparently, a Super Power somewhere "above" who controls the weather, watches over the consequences of sex, plays a leading role in setting prices at the gas pump, and has a particular passion for professional sports. How much sense does that make to you?

But, of course, the question of God goes much deeper than off-hand comments we might be tempted to chalk off to egotism, ignorance or bigotry.

There's no escaping the fact that for several hundred years there's been a slow chipping away at the sense of God's reality, much of it because of the steady advance of scientific knowledge. Whereas once upon a time we might have prayed to a Supreme Being for a good corn crop or better weather, we're more likely nowadays to seed the clouds and scatter fertilizer. When many of us living today were terrified in childhood by the epidemic of polio, it was Salk's vaccine rather than Divine intervention that ended the scourge. Despite a $27 million "Creation Science Museum" in Kentucky that portrays children gamboling with dinosaurs in the Garden of Eden, we turn to biology and geology, not *Genesis*, for a factual account of our origins.[1] It's no wonder that skepticism grows, nicely captured in a child's Sunday School letter to God:

Dear God,
Are you real? Some people don't believe it. If you are, you'd better do something quick.

Many might identify with a *New Yorker* cartoon showing a parishioner shaking hands with his minister after a Sunday

---

[1] But in contrast to fundamentalist attacks on evolutionary biology, progressive Christians are actually celebrating Darwin's birthday each year, as a way of affirming the compatibility of science and religion. Some 13,000 clergy have signed a letter to that effect, and in February, 2010, 861 congregations in all 50 states and 13 countries celebrated Evolution Weekend.

service, saying, "Oh, I know He works in mysterious ways, but if I worked that mysteriously I'd get fired."

But it's not simply science that has chipped away at the traditional image of God; biblical scholarship has played an equally important role. Scholars of the Bible have made it clear that it was not handed down from on high, but coalesced over more than a thousand years. The Bible is, in fact, not really *a* book, but a *library* of books. Although it contains some of the earliest historical writings, it also contains myth, legend, parable, short story, poetry, essay, letters, and so forth; and any "science" is the science of the times and places in which it was written. In the book of *Isaiah* we read that God is "he who sits above the circle of the earth, and its inhabitants are like grasshoppers...." If you read those words literally, you must imagine a being who is closer to earth than you are when you take a commuter flight—you can't see people at all at 15,000 feet! And unless we are going to try to perceive the world as our forebears did in the first century, or fifth, or fifteenth, we're going to have to think critically about what we read in the Bible (or any other ancient sacred literature) rather than receive it as Divine revelation.

Is it really true that there is a God who dwells in Heaven, records the sins and virtues of his subjects, rewards the faithful with eternal life and the wicked with Hell, answers prayers, and intervenes every now and again to change the course of history through miraculous deeds? Did he really open a path through the sea for Moses, send down fire for Elijah, raise Jesus from the dead, and set a day for final Judgment? It is not sacrilegious, but simply intelligent, to question such inherited ideas. Let's face it: for increasing numbers of people, these old beliefs are like antique furniture kept in the attic—still cherished, gazed at nostalgically from time to time, but never brought downstairs, because they would clash with the new furniture.

And so it is not an atheist critic of religion, but a Christian theologian, Gordon Kaufman, who raises the critical question: "The central and most problematical issue for Christian faith and theology is to find a way to make intelligible once again our talk about God, or else give it up."

Two Cheers for Skepticism

There's a story of Wonderland's Alice meeting the White Queen, who told her that she was 101 years, five months and a day old.

"I can't believe *that!*" said Alice.

"Can't you?" the Queen said in a pitying tone. "Try again; draw a long breath, and shut your eyes."

Alice laughed. "There's no use trying," she said. "One *can't* believe impossible things."

"I dare say you haven't had much practice," said the Queen. "When I was your age I always did it for half an hour a day. Why, sometimes I've believed as many as six impossible things before breakfast."

Unfortunately, that's the view that many people hold of religion—that it's a matter of trying to believe "six impossible things before breakfast." The spiritual life is not about trying to believe the unbelievable. In fact, a vital aspect of spirituality is bringing a skeptical intelligence to our evaluation of religious claims.

For example, in recent years the *Chicago Tribune* featured two reports of "religious" findings in the metropolitan region. One of them told of an appearance of the Virgin Mary. Crowds gathered in a Kennedy Expressway underpass, where a salt stain from a leaky crack, according to believers, formed an image of the Blessed Mother. Flowers, candles, and family photos formed an altar to what some dubbed "Our Lady of the Underpass." In the other story, a Muslim man described finding in his backyard a piece of bark in which insects had inscribed the name *Muhammad* in Arabic—"guidance from God, of course," he said. Such stories, rather like the periodic sightings of the image of Jesus in cloud formations, seem to proliferate in times of social stress. Is it a sin to hear them skeptically, especially when the "evidence" offered seems clear only to those predisposed to find it so?

A vocal critic of religion, Daniel Dennett, writes of "the gauze curtains of soft-focus veneration through which we traditionally inspect religion" and of "a traditional exemption from certain sorts of analysis and criticism." Certainly, he and other such critics are right to complain that too often religious views—however outrageous they may seem—are regarded as immune to public challenge. But why should they be? After all, two of the most important questions we can ask in this life are, *What do you mean?* and *How do you know?* And those questions are as fairly raised about religious assertions as they are about assertions in politics, economics, or any other area of human concern. The late astronomer and popularizer of science, Carl Sagan, was right: "Skeptical scrutiny is the means, in both science and religion, by which deep insights can be winnowed from deep nonsense."

Another outspoken critic of religion, Christopher Hitchens, writes, "We do not rely solely upon science and reason, because these are necessary rather than sufficient factors, but we distrust anything that contradicts science or outrages reason." That would seem to be an honoring of skeptical inquiry that any seriously spiritual person could agree with. Doubt, rather like a bulldozer that clears an empty lot of old, dead tree limbs and scattered Coke bottles, so that something new and useful can be built in their place, is an essential first step toward mature spirituality.

But of course, the skepticism that is often expressed about religion goes much deeper than sightings of the Virgin Mary or insects inscribing the name of Muhammad on a branch. For ages, human beings have asked the tough skeptical questions, especially this one: what happens to the idea of a good God in a world that includes not only beauty and love, but tsunamis and suffering?

Some of us grew up singing in Church a favorite hymn, *All Things Bright and Beautiful*. The words go like this:

All things bright and beautiful,
All creatures great and small,
All things wise and wonderful,
The Lord God made them all.

Each little flower that opens,
Each little bird that sings,
God made their glowing colors,

He made their tiny wings.

The purple-headed mountain,
The river running by,
The sunset and the morning,
That brightens up the sky.

The cold wind in the winter,
The pleasant summer sun,
The ripe fruits in the garden,
God made them, every one.

While most of us rejoice in the beauty and wonder of nature celebrated in the hymn, we're also aware of another side to the world we inhabit. That other side is expressed in a *Monty Python's Flying Circus* parody.

All things dull and ugly,
All creatures short and squat,
All things rude and nasty,
The Lord God made the lot;

Each little snake that poisons,
Each little wasp that stings,
He made their brutish venom,
He made their horrid wings.

We may wince even as we laugh at such a potent critique of our often too sentimental view of God, nature, and our life. When we watch cats toy with mice or killer whales toss baby seals before making lunch of them, we probably aren't moved to add a new verse about God's "wise and wonderful" works. Our Victorian forebears, dedicated to the idea that Nature was full of evidence of God's design, tried hard to read moral lessons into even the most (humanly speaking) ghastly evolutionary outcomes. They were troubled, for example, by the Ichneumon wasp, which lays its eggs on or inside of a hapless host—a grasshopper or cricket, perhaps—leaving its larvae to munch on the often paralyzed victim, organ by organ, until it finally dies. Even Darwin was horrified by what evolution had wrought, but some Christian moralists managed to celebrate the gruesomeness as evidence of the wasp mother's love and wise provision for her unborn offspring.

But if we are to have a mature and authentic religion, we shall have to let go of sentimentality and take into account the ugliness and the terror of life, as well as its wonder and beauty.

But why just *two* cheers for skepticism?

Because our skepticism doesn't go deep enough. We need to be skeptical not only about the claims of religion, but also about the critique of it, for both reason and science are inadequate to satisfy the hungers of the heart. Consider, for example, that the bankers, regulators, and Federal Reserve overseers who led us into national financial disaster were among "the best and the brightest." Or that the engineers of BP, skilled at drawing up oil from the depths of the sea, presided over an ecological catastrophe. Reason and science do not save humans from either greed or foolishness. Reason can easily become the rationalization of bad behavior, and science can be turned to purposes which are detrimental to human life. We need to be as skeptical of overblown hymns to science and reason as we are of those to religion.

A noted scientist and Nobel laureate in Physics, Steven Weinberg, has argued that "the world needs to wake up from its long nightmare of religious belief." Yet he is also the man who famously wrote, in a 1977 book entitled *The First Three Minutes*, that "the more the universe seems comprehensible, the more it also seems pointless." *Comprehensible* is a scientific judgment, but *pointless* is a spiritual judgment. What gives the scientist special standing to pronounce on the meaningfulness of our existence? Most of us intuitively experience life as having meaning and worth. Finding words adequate to express such intuition may be difficult, but we trust it. And that trust in our experience of life's meaningfulness lies at the root of religion.

> Reason and science do not save humans from either greed or foolishness.

We need to be skeptical when critics of religion, in the name of reason, become irrational. For example, Christopher Hitchens' recent book, *God is Not Great*, has as the subtitle *Religion Poisons Everything*. At one point in the book, Hitchens expresses his respect and admiration for Martin Luther King, Jr., whose work on behalf of social justice he greatly values. Yet because he is convinced that "religion poisons everything," he cannot accept the spiritual basis of King's ministry. And so he concludes that "in no real as opposed to nominal sense, then, was he a Christian." Further, writing of Dietrich Bonhoeffer, the prominent Protestant theologian who was part of the plot against Hitler, he argues that his religious belief had "mutated into an admirable, but nebulous, humanism." So here we have a critic of religion telling us that two of the most influential figures in twentieth century Christianity were really not Christians at all. That is simply intellectually dishonest, and detracts from the sensible criticisms that Hitchens elsewhere offers.

A wiser response is offered by another atheist critic of religion, Sam Harris:

> "The fact that we must rely on certain intuitions to answer ethical questions does not in the least suggest that there is anything insubstantial, ambiguous, or culturally contingent about ethical truth. ...The Golden Rule really does capture many of our intuitions here. We treat those we

love more or less the way we would like to be treated ourselves. ...Hate, envy, spite, disgust, shame—these are not sources of happiness, personally or socially. Love and compassion are."

With such words (despite his hostility to fundamentalist versions of religion) Harris moves very close to what great religious leaders like Jesus and the Buddha have always taught: there is a sacred dimension to human experience that nourishes just and compassionate behavior. That dimension of human experience cannot be chalked off to mere superstition.

And so, only "two cheers" for skepticism, because finally we need to be skeptical of our skepticism. We must avoid an easy cynicism that misses what is authentic in religious experience. A Christian missionary once said, "My critics are the unpaid watchmen of my soul." And so we need to listen to the critics of religion, but not take them with absolute seriousness; for beyond our skepticism lies a truth which, if only fragmentary and partially understood, nonetheless can provide the basis for a meaningful life.

The Recovery of Reverence

Let's take a journey, in imagination, from Earth to the ends of the universe.

We will have to travel at the speed of light, which is about 11 million miles per minute. At that rate, in less than two seconds we will pass the moon, and in a mere five hours we will escape our solar system. At this incredible speed, 186,000 miles per second, it will take us about four years before we pass the nearest star. As we race through our Milky Way galaxy, we will pass a star about every five years. It will take us about 80,000 years to get all the way across our galaxy, with its 100 billion stars or so. Hoping for enough rest areas along the way, we must travel another 2 million years before we reach the next galaxy, Andromeda. Proving that scientists *do* have a sense of humor, Andromeda is one of what is called our "local group" of seventeen galaxies. If we want to reach the largest group known to us, Hercules (which contains some 10,000 galaxies) we must journey on for another 300 million years. (Recently, the Hubble telescope made a new, freshly mind-boggling discovery: in a very tiny dark and "empty" slice of space, about equal to a single grain of sand held out at arm's length, it found some 1,500 more galaxies, each with 100 billion stars or so, that had never been seen before. That one sighting by Hubble caused astronomers to multiply by five their estimate of the size of the universe.) Enough travel for you?

As we shake our heads in awe at what we now know of the universe, we may well identify with our ancestor whose sense of wonder is memorialized in Scripture:

> "When I look at your heavens, the work of your fingers, the moon and the stars that you have established; what are human beings, that you are mindful of them? Mortals, that you care for them?" (*Psalm* 8)

We earlier mentioned the scientist Carl Sagan, who never tired of talking of those "billions and billions" of stars and galaxies, or of calling you and me "star stuff" because the atoms that make us up—the iron in our blood, the calcium in our bones, the carbon in our brains—were manufactured in giant red stars thousands of light years away in space and billions of years ago in time. "Whenever I think about any of these discoveries,"

Sagan wrote, "I feel a tingle of exhilaration. My heart races. I can't help it... Nearly every scientist has experienced in a moment of discovery or sudden understanding a reverential astonishment." In *The Varieties of Scientific Experience*, he wrote: "The word 'religion' comes from the Latin for 'binding together,' to connect that which has been sundered apart. It's a very interesting concept. And in this sense of seeking the deepest interrelations among things that superficially appear to be sundered, the objectives of religion and science, I believe, are identical or very nearly so."

Reverential astonishment. In those words of Sagan, science and spirituality embrace. No wonder the Catholic scientist and theologian Teilhard de Chardin could write, "Whatever may be said, our century is religious— probably more religious than any other. How could it fail to be so, with such vast horizons opening and such problems to be solved? The only thing is that our age has not yet got the God it can adore."

Our spiritual search is about letting go of gods that are too small.

That's what our spiritual search is about: letting go of gods that are too small, finding a God we can adore. Once we abandon childish images, we have a chance to grow into a more mature spirituality, one that begins in simple reverence. Having faced the skeptical questions that life in all its ambiguity poses for us, we are left—if we are open to our world—with awe and wonder. This new reverence is not bowing before a celestial Monarch, an "Almighty God, King of the universe." Nor does it imply a "wormy" view of ourselves, as expressed in a traditional prayer of confession: "There is no health in us...miserable offenders." The reverence we experience is amazement before the wonder and mystery of life, and gratitude that we are, however briefly, part of it. And this sense of awe and wonder is the cornerstone of all authentic religion.

Unfortunately, much in current culture conspires to dull our sense of wonder, to leave us oblivious. Our separation from the natural world, our excessive busyness, our multitasking, our alienation from other people, dull us to the amazingness of existence. Sensitive commentators outside the religious community often speak eloquently about this "lostness." Douglas Adams, for example, author of *The Hitchhiker's Guide to the Universe*, writes, "The fact that we live at the bottom of a deep gravity well on the surface of a gas-covered planet going around a nuclear fireball 90 million miles away and think this to be <u>normal</u> is obviously some indication of how skewed our perspective tends to be." A stage director in New York City, Brian Kulick, writes, "To me the core of theater and religion is the same: how do you stay in a perpetual state of wonder?" As Albert Einstein put it, "The most beautiful thing we can experience is the mysterious. It is the source of all true art and science. He to whom this emotion is a stranger, who can no longer pause to wonder and stand rapt in awe, is as good as dead: his eyes are closed."

But you, surely, are not as good as dead. Odds are, you have experienced reverential astonishment in the ordinary round of your own life. You may have found it in the experience of wildness in the natural world, or like the Psalmist looking up at the stars at night. You may have known it in the kiss of a lover, or while holding a newborn baby, during a healing conversation, in exuberant exercise or play, or while listening to a Mozart horn concerto. There is no limit to what may elicit our sense of reverence. If you want to grow as a spiritual person, begin by simply trusting such experiences, which move us beyond our skeptical questions to deep intuition about the meaningfulness of life.

The composer Aaron Copland once suggested that "the whole problem can be stated quite simply by asking, 'Is there a meaning to music?' My answer would be, 'Yes.' And 'Can you state in so many words what the meaning is?' My answer to that would be, 'No.'" But just as the meaningfulness of music—or art, love, beauty—is obvious to us even though we get tongue-tied trying to explain it, so is our trust in the meaningfulness of life, which is what *faith* means. Faith is not about believing certain doctrines—Virgin Birth, atonement, whatever; it is a trusting confidence about our place in the cosmos. Religion, it has been wisely said, *is not a way of looking at certain things, but a certain way of looking at all things.* Religion—or spirituality—is a focused attitude of trust that moves us to an ethical lifestyle that becomes our "thank-you note" for the gift of being here.

Of course, the reverence of which we speak does not depend upon the traditional image of a Supreme Being who is somewhere "out there" sorting through prayers and working the levers of human history. The former Secretary-General of the United Nations, Dag Hammarskjöld, left behind a journal of spiritual reflections after his death, in which he reflected, "God does not die on the day we cease to believe in a personal deity…but we die on the day that our lives cease to be illumined by the steady radiance, renewed daily, of a wonder, the source of which is beyond all reason."

That discovery, of wonder beyond all reason, is at the heart of the spiritual life.

We Are the Tradition

Diana Athill, a respected British literary figure, in her eighties wrote a delightful memoir *Somewhere Towards the End* in which, though an unbeliever, she expressed her appreciation of the tradition in which she grew up.

> "So we, the irreligious, live within social structures built by the religious. And however critical or resentful we may be of parts of them,

no honest atheist would deny that insofar as the saner aspects of religion hold in a society, that society is the better for it. We take a good nibble of our brother's cake before throwing it away.

Right behaviour, to me, is the behaviour taught me by my Christian family: one should do unto one's neighbour as one would like him to do unto one, should turn the other cheek, should not pass on the other side of those in trouble, should be gentle to children, should avoid obsession with material possessions. I have accepted a great deal of Christ's teaching, partly because it was given me in childhood by people I loved and partly because it continues to make sense, and the nearer people come to observing it the better I like them (not that they come—or ever have come—very near it, and nor have I). So my piece of my brother's cake is a substantial chunk...."

Athill's gracious attitude toward a religious upbringing, much of which she now rejects, is a good guide to the way we might look at the Judeo-Christian tradition that most of us have inherited. We need not accept the whole of it in order to affirm its ethical and spiritual core.

Think, for example, of our contemporary approach to the Bible. We can be quite clear that it is not a divine hand-me-down, a compendium of God's own directions for our living. The Bible is, rather, the "family scrapbook" of a particular human community reflecting on its experience over a great period of time. The Greek title *ta biblia* actually means "the books." So, as we have noted, the Bible is not *a* book, but a whole library of books written over at least a thousand year period, and consisting of a variety of genres: history, parable, myth, legend, letters, sermons, proverbs, songs, short stories, and so forth. These disparate works must be read against the setting—historical, cultural, literary—of the times and places in which they were written. We get into big trouble when we try to interpret texts without context.

Nonetheless, we have similar questions to those which troubled our forebears in generations past: Where did the world come from? What is our place in it? What should we live for? Why is there suffering? What—if anything—lies beyond our death? Many of their answers are outmoded for us, having arisen in a universe vastly smaller than the one we now perceive. But we can respect our ancestors' questions and we can honor their search. We can, in the words of one wise observer, "Take from the altar of the past the fire, not the ashes."

Daniel Dennett, an academic critic of religion, particularly in its dogmatic forms, has written, "Just as the Latin minds of ancient Rome gave way to French and Italian and Spanish minds, Christian minds of today are quite unlike the minds of the earliest Christians. The major religions of today are as different from their ancestral versions as today's music is different from the music of ancient Greece and Rome." We should not be surprised that religions, like all else in human society, evolve and change over time. Yet we may discover what Harry Emerson Fosdick, a theologian of the last century, called "abiding truth in changing categories." Despite all of our differences from those who lived two or three thousand years ago, we share certain common experiences. We know, as they did, that we are dependent beings in a universe not of our making, which we experience as both nurturing and threatening.

We sense, as they did, that the Other with whom (or which) we have to deal can be trusted. We share certain core convictions: that existence is good after all, not a cosmic joke; that we belong here (as "star stuff" to Sagan, "image of God" to the Bible); that compassion and love are our finest purpose. Such core intuitions are more than enough to provide us with a life agenda, whether we live in the first or the fifteenth or the twenty-first century.

So we are both heirs of an ancient tradition and bearers of it to those who come after us. Spiritual seeking did not begin with us, and it certainly will not end with us. We have a legacy to leave, and must not be afraid to imagine it afresh. We need not feel intimidated by those who claim exclusive ownership of the tradition, whose pamphlets offer "four steps in the plan of salvation" or for whom "atonement in the Blood" requires our assent. It is enough for us to witness to our fragmentary yet enlivening sense of the Sacred "in whom we live and move and have our being."

Meeting the Sacred in Stories

This Sacred Mystery has been recognized, in however varied forms, from time immemorial. To illustrate, take a look at four stories, from the Jewish, Christian and Hindu traditions, and from a contemporary writer. In doing so, understand that the language of religious tradition is often the language not of science or history, but of story. If we listen to these stories with a literalism that is peculiar to the modern age, we will miss much of their wisdom. Instead of asking, "Is this really true?"— meaning factually or scientifically accurate—listen for a deeper meaning. All of us recognize that a good novel may tell us more about our human journey than a psychology textbook. It is exactly in this sense that many religious tales have wisdom to offer us, if we only have ears to hear.

The Jewish story comes from the book of *Exodus*, a story of Moses in conversation with God. Moses is presented in the tradition as one who spoke with God face to face, as a man speaks with a friend. He is also the leader of a contentious group of migrants, and in the scene we are recounting he insists that his God (*Yahweh* was his name) show him his "glory," (the luminous presence of the Deity) as assurance that he will accompany Moses on the journey. In reply, Yahweh says to Moses, "I'll tell you what I'm going to do. I will make my goodness pass before you and I will pronounce before you my name, Yahweh. And I will be gracious to whom I will be gracious. But you may not see my face." Yahweh then, in the story, takes Moses and places him in a cleft in the cliff. As he passes by he covers Moses with his hand, and then when he is past he takes his hand away so that Moses may see his back, but, he says, "My face shall not be seen." Can you imagine a clearer way to say that all human perception of God is partial, that the Sacred is beyond our ever fully knowing?

The Christian story comes from the Gospels (Matthew, Mark, Luke and John.) It is, in fact, the *only* story before the last week of Jesus' life that they all tell—and it shows up in six different versions! So obviously it is heavy with significance. The story is that Jesus is teaching a huge throng of people out in the "wilderness"—four or five thousand men (only *men* get numbered in that patriarchal society!) plus women and children, and the teaching goes on so long that everybody's getting hungry and there's no possible way to scrounge up enough food to feed them. So at Jesus' urging his close followers manage to come up with a few loaves of bread and a couple of fish, which Jesus blesses and tells them to distribute. Lo and behold!—not only do all in this throng of thousands eat till they're full, but they even collect baskets of leftovers!

Now, what are we to make of that story? Some say, "Well, of course it was a miracle!" Others rationalize, "No, it's just that once somebody offered to share his lunch, others brought theirs out also." In reality, there are multiple layers of meaning—more than we can unpack here. But the heart of it is this: anthropologists tell us that once you know what the eating rules are in a society—who is allowed to eat with whom—you can infer just about everything else about that society. And what we know for certain is that the rule-makers in Jesus' society were furious at the way he broke the rules—eating with "sinners" (the religiously nonobservant as well as flagrantly immoral), mixing social classes at the same table, associating with women and children, touching the sick and disfigured. That wilderness meal—whatever actually happened historically—symbolizes Jesus' practice of inviting all sorts and conditions of people to eat together in community, violating the most basic rules of purity and social separation.

If all of this sounds like a long ago fuss about obscure Jewish ritual rules, think back to the beginning of the civil rights movement in our own country. In the early 1960s our society was convulsed when some black young people dared to sit down at a "whites only" lunch counter. Some of them had ketchup poured over them and lighted cigarettes snuffed out on their necks—such was the rage over a challenge to eating customs. Here in modern, democratic America we had *laws* about who could eat with whom and, just as the anthropologists argued, the segregated lunch counter was a miniature model of our society as a whole. When young people, black and white, ate together or rode the same bus, they were challenging an entire system in the name of a different vision of how we should live together. And that is exactly what Jesus was doing—and what all those "eating and drinking" stories are about. He was replacing the segregated table with an inclusive table, a symbol of a whole new vision of society in which—as his follower Paul later put it—"There is no longer Jew or Greek, there is no longer slave or free, there is no longer male and female; for all of you are one in Christ Jesus."

The story from the Hindu tradition concerns Krishna, who is thought of rather as many Christians think of Jesus—as one who is both a real historical figure and also God incarnate. Diana Eck, a student of Hindu thought, tells one much-loved story, of Krishna as cowherd calling a group of milkmaids to the forest in the middle of the night to dance a great circle dance. When they arrive, Krishna miraculously multiplies himself (another "miracle of multiplication!") so as to be able to dance with each and every one of them. There is, in other words, plenty of Krishna to go around, an abundance of sacred presence. But as soon as the milkmaids become possessive, each one thinking that Krishna is dancing with her alone, he disappears. Now, what is that story about? Certainly it also could be read (as gospel stories often are) as a straightforward miracle story: Krishna, being God, can multiply himself at will. But surely you are able to hear that story as symbolic, a vivid way of saying that the sacred is available to each and all, but is lost to us when we suppose that God is our exclusive possession, unavailable to those "others."

The final story, much briefer, is told by the novelist David Foster Wallace. "There are," he says, "these two young fish swimming along, and they happen to meet an older fish swimming the other way who nods at them and says, 'Morning, boys. How's the water?' And the two young fish go swimming on for a bit, until eventually one of them looks over at the other and asks, 'What the hell is water?'"

In these symbolic stories, we are reminded that God can never fully be perceived, dreams of community in which "otherness" disappears, can never be the private possession of any individual, and—rather than being a separate Being "out there somewhere"—is the Context of all existence, the Ocean in which we swim.

Chapter 2

Our Hunger to Be Real Persons

One of our deep hungers is the need to be ourselves—to be real, not fake persons. In our best moments, we aspire to have integrity, not simply fill a role, to be useful, not just take up space during our brief stay on the planet. We have a deep-rooted need to be authentic, not just a reflection of other people's expectations.

But if we no longer trust that there is some authority—whether Book or Church—with inside information on the Divine will, what are we to trust? And if we no longer picture God as the Great Parent who hands down the rules of the household, how do we know how to behave? What does it mean to live a "good life" without absolute external rules? What might it look like to be a person of spiritual integrity in the twenty-first century?

Becoming Two-Pocket People

The influential Jewish sage Martin Buber often told the story of a Hasidic master who said that we human beings should always have two pockets to reach into according to our need. In the right pocket should be these words: "For my sake, the world was created." In the left pocket should be these: "I am dust and ashes." Perhaps spiritual wisdom begins with accepting both of these truths about ourselves.

"I am dust and ashes." This is a recognition that we are part of the natural order—dependent creatures, weak, fragile, and vulnerable. We are limited in knowledge, full of earthy impulses, interconnected with all other creatures. As vulnerable creatures, we face threats and sufferings. And as part of nature we cannot count on a God of Special Favors who will inevitably rescue us from the threats of being human. As Jesus said, "God sends sun to shine on the evil and on the good, and rain to fall on the just and on the unjust." Nature is not only the warm sun caressing our skin, but the tsunami sweeping to watery death the bad and good alike. If we are to continue to speak of God, we

must include both—Divine indifference along with Divine caring. "We are dust and ashes."

On the other hand, *"For me the world was created."* That is, we also experience the universe as nourishing and embracing us, making us glad to be alive, in experiences that enable us to speak of the "love of God." Perhaps we have known the quite astonishing yet not uncommon feeling of being accepted by that which is greater than we—whether or not we name it God—an experience which encourages us to receive this vulnerable life not as a bad joke or a puzzle to be solved, but as a gift. We become conscious of having a certain dignity, grounded in nature but transcending it—to explore, to be creative, to show compassion, to love. And we accept the responsibility that goes with that dignity, to be caretakers, trustees, of the planet we inhabit. "For us the world was created."

Spiritual wisdom begins with accepting our being as "two-pocket people," at one with all the rest of nature, yet possessing a particular dignity as human beings.

Are You at Home with Yourself?

It's not an easy piece of work to know who we are, to be comfortable in our own skin, at home with both our creatureliness and our spirituality. For the most part, we accept the image of ourselves that our culture and upbringing give to us. We tend to be a walking collage of bits and pieces that we have picked up from the expectations of others. Oftentimes we feel that others don't really know us, and might be disappointed or even shocked if they did. And we ourselves may be afraid to look very deeply within for fear of what we might discover. These fears are born in our failure to understand and accept the two realities about ourselves, that we are earthy creatures with spiritual strivings. That word of Augustine still speaks for many: "Our hearts are always restless, until in You they rest."

Not long ago, the author David James Duncan spoke to an interviewer about his childhood religious upbringing, much of which he had tossed aside. Yet something in his life seemed to be missing. But finally, he said, he experienced a certain "hollowing out, after years of effort, a little place in my heart about the size of a thimble." And then it suddenly happened that "when I was twenty, in India one day, I turned to God with embarrassed sincerity and said, 'Would you care to fill this little thimble with anything?' And instantaneously—almost absurdly really—an undeniable, unimaginable, indescribable lake of peace and love landed on my head in reply." Duncan admitted to a certain embarrassment in telling his story. "The problem with talking about spiritual experiences is that [they] by definition…transcend language, so you end up sounding like a fool. The problem with *not* talking about spiritual experiences, though, is that they're the events for which I'm most grateful. The paradox: would I rather sound like a fool, or an ingrate?"

> When love breaks through, we are suddenly able to accept our weaknesses and faults without coming unglued.

Well, it's not foolish to acknowledge such experiences, for many share them. The sense of being accepted by the Other that is both beyond and within us is what the Christian tradition has called "grace." That experience breaks into the anxiety, confusion and self-doubt that trouble us, and frees us to journey along a path toward becoming a real self. Of course, the experience need not be as dramatic as Duncan's. We need not be "born again;" we live in God's grace simply by virtue of having been *born*. Whether for us the breakthrough comes as we look up at the stars, ponder the mysteries of DNA, find someone who loves us, help heal another's hurt, or take a risk for justice, the experience of being accepted restores us to our real selves.

And the paradox is this: that when such love breaks through, we are suddenly able to accept our weakness and faults without coming unglued. We come to accept the fact that even our best impulses are tainted by self-interest, that we pretend to know more than we really know and to "have it all together" when we really don't. We begin to see that our strengths are also our pitfalls: ambition that enables us to achieve can also result in a stunted personal life with no time for leisure or friendship, appreciation or love; the pride that enables us to walk in dignity may also keep us from being able to acknowledge our mistakes; the charm that opens doors for us may lapse into shallowness on which we depend—no deepening, no growth, no newness; the intellect in which we trust may mask a denial of the emotions, which one day erupt in us with discomfiting force. The wonder of the grace which enables us to accept ourselves is that we are increasingly able to see ourselves as we really are without despair.

The Trappist monk Thomas Merton, in recounting a personal experience, captures the experience of many of us:

> "In Louisville, at the corner of Fourth and Walnut, in the center of the shopping district, I was suddenly overwhelmed with the realization that I loved all these people, that they were mine and I theirs, that we could not be alien to one another, even though we were total strangers. It was like waking from a dream of separateness, of spurious self-isolation in a special world, a world of renunciation and supposed holiness.... This sense of liberation from an illusory difference was such a relief and such a joy to me that I almost laughed out loud. And I suppose my happiness could have taken form in the words;

'Thank God, thank God that I <u>am</u> like other men—that I am only [one person] among others.'"

Feeding Our Wolves

A mother came by surprise upon her young son, who was old enough to know better, pulling up flowers in the family garden and tossing them aside. He jumped when he saw her and immediately said, "This isn't really me, Mommy!"

The child's response to being caught doing what he knew was wrong is a kind of parable of our human life. We are caught wondering about the "really me," and we're quick to blame others for whatever predicaments we may find ourselves in. It is this characteristic that moved Anna Russell to write a "Psychiatric Folksong."

At three I had a feeling of
Ambivalence towards my brothers
And so it follows naturally
That I poisoned all my lovers.

But now I'm happy; I have learned
The lesson this has taught
That everything I do that's wrong
Is someone else's fault.

Of course, there's a certain amount of truth to our avoidance of responsibility by pointing the finger at other persons or influences. After all, we didn't get to pick our genes, our parents, our neighborhood, our culture—and probably not our religion either. So we are less free than we are sometimes inclined to imagine, subject to myriad influences from birth till death. Nonetheless, the same evolutionary process that has bequeathed us both aggressive and compassionate impulses, both selfishness and altruism, has also given us the power to make choices, to decide which impulses to nurture and which to suppress. At some point in our lives, given all the influences that have affected us, we need to say, "This is who I am. This is the way I choose to live. I will make my decisions, and I will be responsible to live with the consequences of them." At the end of the day, we can't pawn off our responsibility on our surroundings, our parents, our genes, a devil or God.

A story from Native American tradition tells of an Indian elder talking to his son about life's meaning.

> "There are, living within each of us," he said, "two wolves who are fighting to the death. One of them says to us, 'You are part of the tribe, and what you do or don't do will affect our community. So live in harmony with others. Work together to solve problems. Care for the weak. Love and be kind to our mother earth. Live at peace.' The other wolf is saying, 'Don't worry about the tribe; look out for yourself. You have to get ahead, even if it requires shunning the weak. Don't worry about nature. Use nature, that's what it's for. Be concerned with yourself. The others are rivals and enemies.'"

At that, the young boy looked up with big, worried eyes into the elder's face and said, "But father, which wolf will win?" And the answer came, "Whichever one you feed, my son. Whichever one you feed."

And that is the human story in all its ambiguity, the mixture of good and bad impulses that are ours by nature. We are neither divine creatures nor devils, neither all good nor all evil. We have choice, and which wolf wins depends on which one we choose to feed.

Dusting Off an Antique Word

That antique word, embarrassingly old-fashioned, is "duty."

It's a word that seems alien to our time, which emphasizes feeling good, staying free from commitments, organizing life around ourselves. Perhaps once upon a time the word *duty* meant knuckling under pressures simply to obey authoritative others, or "the will of God." What I mean is quite different: an affirming of duty that arises from an innate sense that it's wrong to suck at the breast of the world without "giving back." It's duty to values that are freely chosen. What are such values? Behaving morally, even when no one's watching; doing conscientious work, even when we might get by with less; keeping faith with a partner, even during the dry stretches that are a part of all relationships; speaking the truth, preserving nature, acting with regard to the common good. Through such "giving back" we redeem our lives from insignificance.

For most of us, a part of that giving back involves our *work*. We mustn't be sentimental about work; for many, it is a boring, frustrating economic necessity, while for others—the migrant fruit-picker, the sweat shop shirt-sewer—it may be bitter and unjust. But work is more than economic necessity; we all need something to point to as a job well done for a purpose that matters. Of course, even the most useful work has its "just-grind-it-out" moments. But as a wise observer of the human condition has noted, many a task begun in a dry-as-dust sense of duty ends up aglow with devotion. Work is more than what one is paid for; in fact, much of the world's significant work— caring for an elderly relative, volunteering at a food bank—goes without monetary reward at all. Even as we value our own work, it's a useful spiritual discipline to ponder where we would be without the work of others. Whether they collect our trash or teach our children, truck our groceries or fill our potholes, process our social security checks or check our brake fluids, vaccinate our three-year-olds or bury our dead, our lives are unthinkable without them. In our gratitude, we may offer our *own* work as an act of devotion, a way of saying "thank you" for all that sustains our own life.

Duty. Whatever our faults and mistakes, we need to identify what is good and trustworthy in us, celebrate it, and stay true to it. As George Bernard Shaw has a character in one of his plays say, "This is the true joy in life...being a force of nature instead of a feverish, selfish little clot of ailments and grievances, complaining that the world will not devote itself to making you happy." For personal happiness is not so much a direct attainment as it is the by-product of responsible living.

"Don't Just Do Something..."

Becoming spiritually mature takes practice.

No surprises there. You may have innate musical ability, but you'll not play violin with the Cleveland Orchestra without practice, practice, practice. You may love baseball, but you won't play second base for the Cubs without practice, practice, practice. Whether you aspire to competence as a dry cleaner, legal aide, auto mechanic, or computer programmer, you'll have lessons to learn and skills to master. And so with the spiritual life: it takes practice and—to use another antique word—discipline.

Of the many practices that lead to a deeper spiritual life, the most important is simply *taking time* to let your soul catch up with your body. The fancy word for it is "meditation." As the saying goes, "Don't just *do* something, sit there." Jon Kabat-Zinn, whose book *Wherever You Go, There You Are* is a terrific place to begin, writes, "Making time for meditation each day doesn't mean...that you can't run around or get things done. It means that you are more likely to know what you're doing because you have stopped for a while and watched, listened, understood."

Meditation simply means becoming aware, becoming alert, being fully present to a few moments between sleep and sleep. It is taking time, as one writer puts it, "to discover who *you* are; what feels right and best for you....You need to write your own music, you need to look inside yourself and see what is there....The point is to find your own soul and kick it, poke it with a stick, see if it's still alive, and then watch which way it moves." Such time for quiet personal reflection is desperately needed in our age of constant communication (in the last ten years in the U.S. we've gone from 2.7 to 18 hours a week online and from 12 billion to 247 billion *daily* emails.) We may use cell phones, iPads, email, and Twitter to stay helpfully "in touch" with others, or we may use them as a diversion to keep from getting better acquainted with ourselves.

If you want to begin meditating, start with three minutes a day, then five, then ten, until it becomes a comfortable habit. Try this: whether or not you have a belief in a personal God, try talking out loud to God (or the spirit or the sacred or the universe or just life itself). In your talk, tell how things are really going with you. Go deeper; look over your life in that sacred time and space. Just tell the truth, don't pretend, and don't worry about getting the words right. You may find that you end up at a quite different place than where you began. Whether you call it meditation or centering or prayer or self-discovery, it is a way of becoming acquainted with the depths of your own being.

You may even find, as others have, that the time of quiet meditation leads to laughter. A great theologian of the twentieth century, Reinhold Niebuhr, said, "Humor is a prelude to faith and laughter is the beginning of prayer." Does that sound weird to you? In fact, when we are honest with ourselves in the quiet time we often end up by laughing at our pretensions. Meditation helps restore our lost sense of perspective, which causes us no end of amusement at the seriousness with which we often take ourselves.

So we shouldn't take even our meditation too seriously. One writer says that he needs a book about "when ordinary things happen to average people." We need, he continues, "a spirituality of the uneventful, of the places in one's life that are neither deep nor exhilaratingly high." As the old mountain lady once said, "The trouble with life is it's so *daily*." Remember: meditation need not be fancy, our gratitude may be for simple things, and our deepened awareness may be of the wonder of the ordinary.

> When we are honest with ourselves, we often end up laughing at our pretensions.

Christina Rossetti once wrote of her fear of not having someone in particular to thank for the blessings of life: "Were there no God, we would be in this glorious world with grateful hearts and no one to thank." Whether or not you have Someone to thank, don't put off making gratitude the center of your time of meditation. To be grateful is at the heart of a spiritual life. To know gratitude is to know that we already have plenty and need not strain to get more, that it's more important to be useful than to be rich. Gratitude is the very heart of spiritual living.

We might well speak of many other avenues to a deepened spirituality. We might speak of *play*, so important in a time when we live in an entertainment society, substituting others' amusements for our own. We might speak about reconnecting with *nature*, as great sages like Jesus have always taught us: "Consider the lilies of the field, how they grow...." If a sunset, for example, happened only once a year, the whole world would take chairs outside to sit and watch, yet how few of us pause to notice this everyday wonder. Or we might speak about *humor* and its role in healing our stressed lives. One university studied a group of medical students who watched a comedian on video, and within thirty minutes their disease-fighting white cells had increased by 25%. (A professor in that school added, "If we took what we now know about laughter and bottled it, it would require FDA approval.") Or we might speak of all the *small tasks* that restore our flagging spirits—fixing something, cleaning the yard, reading a book, talking to a neighbor.

All this is to say that spiritual practices are nothing esoteric or strange, just ways of *paying attention*—to what's going on inside us, with other people, and in our world. And our basic need is still caught in this advice: "Don't do something, *just sit there*."

"Don't Cry Because It's Over..."

One of the major themes of orthodox Christian faith is captured in words of Saint Paul: "If for this life only we have hoped in Christ, we are of all people most to be pitied...if the dead are not raised, 'let us eat and drink, for tomorrow we die.'"

Does that argument—that if we can expect no life beyond this one, we may as well just live it up—make sense to you? Do we live responsibly and caringly because we hope for heaven or fear hell? No. Our life has its own intrinsic value—value that is only enhanced by its brevity. The attempt to live a truthful, just, and loving life offers its own satisfactions, without worrying about piling up points for Judgment Day.

The historian Arnold Toynbee wrote about an uncle who had died at age thirty and who had written before his death, "We lift our heads for one moment above the waves, give one wild glance around, and perish. But that glance, was it for nothing?" Most of us want to cry out, "Oh no, it was not for nothing!" The faith that we have is confidence that this life is meaningful and worthwhile, and doesn't require a life beyond this one to validate it.

The Christian religion that is dominant in Western culture has made a mistake in locating the mystery of being beyond death. The mystery is *life*—the wonder that anything is, instead of not being. It seems obvious that we, like all other creatures, come into being, grow, flourish, decline and die, leaving others to carry on the grand experiment of life. The tragedy, as Norman Cousins has written, "is not death, but what dies inside us while we live." Or, as Rabbi Joshua Loth Liebman puts it, "Death is not the enemy of life, but its friend. For it is the knowledge that our years are limited which makes them so precious. It is the truth that time is but lent to us which makes us, at our best, look upon our years as a trust handed into our temporary keeping." To live in such appreciation takes grown-up courage; unlike the sense of invulnerability and immortality that youth possess, adults know that our personal existence will come to an end.

In a commencement address at Stanford University, Steve Jobs, the CEO of Apple Computer, told a story about his own coming to terms with death. When he was seventeen he came across a quotation that went like this: "If you live each day as if it was your last, someday you'll most certainly be right." "It made an impression on me," he said, "and since then for the past thirty-three years I have looked in the mirror every morning and asked myself, 'If today were the last day of my life, would I want to do what I am about to do today?' And whenever the answer has been 'no' for too many days in a row, I know I need to change something." He went on, "Your time is limited. So don't waste it living someone else's life. Don't be trapped by dogma—which is living with the results of other people's thinking. Don't let the noise of others' opinions drown out your own inner voice. And most important, have the courage to follow your heart and intuition. They somehow already know what you truly want to become. Everything else is secondary."

An old Jewish proverb speaks the truth about our human situation: "Every person knows that they must die, but no one believes it." It is a part of spiritual maturity not only to know it, but to believe it, to accept this life as the gift and mystery that it is, to live it to the fullest for the sake not only of our own happiness, but for the common good. Someone has said—wisely, I think—"Don't cry because it's over. Smile because it happened." That acceptance is part of what it means to be mature.

A major problem with much religious thought is that it is unnecessarily complex and obscure. The writer Aldous Huxley got to the heart of what life is about: "It is a bit embarrassing to have been concerned with the human problem all one's life and find at the end that one has no more to offer by way of advice than 'try to be a little kinder.'" Or as the philosopher Bertrand Russell, hardly an orthodox believer, wrote, "The root of the matter is a very simple and old-fashioned thing, a thing so simple that I am almost ashamed to mention it for fear of the derisive smile with which wise cynics will greet my words. The thing I mean—please forgive me for mentioning it—is love or compassion. If you feel this, you have a motive for existence, a guide for action, a reason for courage, an imperative necessity for intellectual honesty."

That mention of love takes us beyond our conversation about personal spirituality into our hunger for relationship with other persons, for real community, and that will be the subject of our next chapter.

Chapter 3

Our Hunger for Relationship

One of the deepest hungers of the human heart is to be in satisfying relationships with other people. In a sense, we are not even born human; we become human in our interrelationships, and the character of those relationships either enriches or diminishes us. Unfortunately, we are heirs of a long intellectual tradition of excessive individualism, summed up in Descartes' famous phrase, "I think, therefore I am." A wiser aphorism comes from Africa: "I am, because we are." We are made for community, and when we cannot find it, we know the pain that is called loneliness.

The Pain Called Loneliness

We have two words in English for being alone: *solitude* and *loneliness*. The difference between them is that whereas solitude is a restorative aloneness that we freely choose, loneliness is a deprived aloneness that we wish to escape.

A group of some twenty-five or thirty university students were asked the question, "When have you ever experienced loneliness?" Here are some of their answers:

- *On the first night after moving from home*
- *When I was a new person in a new place*
- *When my troubles stacked up on me, isolating me from others*
- *When I am expressing my political views*
- *When I am upset and no one can understand or care*
- *When I have a different opinion than the rest of the group*
- *When I go to parties, especially big ones*
- *After Mom and Dad broke up*
- *As a single person surrounded by couples*
- *As a newcomer in a group when no one makes an attempt to talk to me*
- *When my grandfather died*
- *After a big celebration, when everyone goes home*
- *When there's a lack of communication with a friend*
- *Last year at Christmas*
- *In a crowd*

These young adults were also asked to complete a sentence, which began, "Loneliness is...." Their definitions included:

- *Feeling like there is no one you can trust completely*
- *When you have joy and love to share, and there is no one with whom to share it*
- *A feeling of emptiness and being scared*
- *Feeling isolated, not fitting in with the norm*
- *Not being able to pick up the phone and call someone when you need to*
- *When those around you don't understand*
- *When being unsure of all of your friendships*

We human beings have no deeper spiritual question than this one: "How do I grow out of loneliness into relationship?"

From "Pit Bull" to Love

One of the weaknesses in Western religion has been a preoccupation with our relationship with the eternal Other while paying less attention to the nearby others with whom we daily live. Yet the wholeness (that's what "salvation" means) that is the goal of religious life always involves discovering the other (called the "neighbor"), valuing the other, rejoicing in the other. The Christian scriptures insist that our connection with the eternal Other and the others around us are intimately connected. As one text puts it, "Those who do not love a brother or sister whom they have seen, cannot love God whom they have not seen." So, the love of God and the love of other people always go together. The "with-ness" for which we long is integral to authentic religious experience.

Some years ago, Lee Atwater, who had been chairman of the Republican National Committee and a key figure in the 1988 election campaign of the first George Bush, who was noted for a "pit-bull style of politics," was back in the news. Only in his forties, he was diagnosed with a brain tumor, which changed his whole perception of life. Having faced the void, Atwater said, "It's going to be hard for me to be as tough on people.... I have a better sense of humanity, a better sense of fellowship with people than I've ever had before." He went on to say, "Forget money and power. I had no idea how wonderful people are. I wish I had known this before. What a way to have to find out." He drastically cut back his usual 12-14 hour workdays on the advice of doctors and discovered that "70% of the things I was frantically pursuing didn't matter anyhow.... The things I didn't think about too much are now important, and that's human relationships and the love of a lot of people and how valuable they are." Before his death, he seems to have discovered what the scientist Carl Sagan once observed: "For small creatures such as we, the vastness is bearable only through love."

From "pit bull" to love. The question is, what does it take, hopefully short of a tumor, to awaken us to loving relationships with other people? And what might that love look like?

What Are We Afraid of?

Moving from loneliness to relationship, from separation to love, can be hard work. One of the biggest barriers to feeding this hunger of the heart seems to be fear. We shrink back from others out of fear of saying the wrong thing, revealing too much of ourselves, giving offense, being rejected, wandering too far out of our comfort zone, making a fool of ourselves.

So the question becomes, what is it that we need to move away from fear and towards other people?

One thing that we need is *to allow ourselves to be known*, to come out of hiding. Part of our problem in relating to other people is that we are partly concealed within the roles we play. We are the college graduate, the dentist, the computer guru, the jokester. We also show only our best side, playing the part of someone who's "got it all together." If we are to get closer to other people, we need to stop hiding from them—and from ourselves. We needn't trumpet all our weaknesses, just face them and, when appropriate, acknowledge them. When we make a mistake, our first tendency is to hide it or to explain it away. It's amazing how it helps relationships when we can simply say, "I made a mistake," or "I'm in a lousy mood—sorry." Our more usual pattern is to judge ourselves by a different standard than we use with other people. Humorously called the use of "irregular verbs," we tend to parse language like this: "*I* am firm in my principles; *you* are somewhat stubborn; *he* is a pig-headed fool." Jesus observed that we ought first to take the log out of our own eye before we offer to remove the splinter from the eye of our neighbor. What we discover when we allow ourselves to be known is that by admitting our frailties and making ourselves vulnerable, we also allow others also to be the imperfect people they are. When together we drop the pretense of always having it together, community becomes possible.

We need to allow ourselves to be known, to come out of hiding.

Besides being honest with and about ourselves, it's crucially important in our nourishing of relationships simply *to pay attention*. One writer caught the difficulty of really *being with* others in our multi-electronic age in these words:

> "We see it all the time. We're on our cell phones talking to someone other than those at the table with us. We're putting somebody on hold while we take another call. We are shuttled by device and distraction to somebody's subroutine. The message is always the same: whoever is calling needs my attention more than you do; whatever

this call concerns, it is more important than the present conversation; whoever is 'out there' is more interesting than this, or you, or now."

How often we do simply half-listen to the other, eager for them to stop talking so we can tell our (much more important!) story. The beginning of relationship with other people is simply to be present and to pay attention.

The Miracle of Listening

Some forty people were gathered for an all-day seminar on communication skills. After the morning presentation, a woman in the group—quite obviously upset and angry—challenged the speaker with an outburst that he couldn't understand. Unable to discern where she was "coming from," he simply acknowledged her comments and moved on. The next part of the seminar included a series of exercises in which people, in twos, talked to one another about controversial issues ranging from abortion to gay rights to the role of religion in politics. One person would express his point of view about the subject, while the other simply listened attentively, and then paraphrased what she or he had heard, to demonstrate to the speaker's satisfaction that they had been understood. Then the two would switch roles. After five or six such "rounds" of careful listening and paraphrasing, the leader of the workshop asked the group what they had learned from that exercise. The previously angry, upset woman was the first to raise her hand. She was now a different person—beaming and confident. "I have never been listened to so carefully in my entire life!" she said. For the rest of the day she was an involved, constructive contributor to the work of the group. The change in her behavior was astonishing. What made the difference? The miracle of being listened to.

The building blocks of good relationships are many, but none is more important than listening. All of us know the hurt and disappointment of being only half-heard when we wanted and needed someone's full attention, and all of *us* have hurt and disappointed *others* in the same way. We see ourselves in a "Hagar the Horrible" cartoon, as his wife pours out her frustration: "You never listen to a thing I say!! NOT A THING! NOT A SINGLE THING!!" To which Hagar responds, staring into space, "Oh, not bad—how was your day?" But it is possible to learn and practice new habits and to experience that same miracle. Our forbears in faith made that discovery several thousand years ago, as reflected in these sayings from the book of *Proverbs:* "Someone who is sure of himself does not talk all the time" and, "A person's thoughts are like water in a deep well, but someone with insight can draw them out."

One way to begin to experience a new way of listening is to *listen to others with an ear to what we can agree with.* That's not our usual mental habit. Ordinarily, we listen to others—particularly when the subject is touchy—only until we find the weakness in the other's point of view, which we can then exploit as we launch into our refutation. It is literally life-changing when we habitually listen to others with the intention of searching out what in the other's point of view we can agree with. Differences remain, of course, but that place of agreement becomes a bridge across which we can walk to meet another on common ground.

In the nation's capital, a dialogue was held on the subject of national defense between a Pentagon official and a critic from a liberal "think tank." But the rule in this dialogue was that after one person had spoken, his opposite party—before presenting his own point of view—had to list all of the things in the previous speaker's presentation with which he agreed. The moderator of the meeting then wrote up all these agreements on a chalkboard for everyone in the audience to see. After the meeting as over, the Pentagon spokesperson was interviewed and he said, "You know, I walk into this meeting and I see that other guy and I say to myself, 'He and I have absolutely nothing in common.' But then I listen to him, and I discover that we agree about eighty percent of the time." Clearly the twenty percent of difference that remains is important. But by listening for what they could agree with in the viewpoint of the other, the "conservative" and the "liberal" built a bridge across which they could walk to meet one another as human beings, rather than as political adversaries. Imagine what our society might look like if that example were to be multiplied! And what works for public figures can work in our day-to-day relationships as well.

Of course, our practice of such communication skills—careful listening, paraphrasing, finding where we can agree—has to be honest. The "love" in "love your neighbor as yourself" means seriously intending the well-being of the other. This kind of love is not an emotion, a feeling, but a decision and commitment to affirm the other. You may have all the communication skills in the world, but if you do not genuinely care about the other, they become merely manipulative. Honestly listening to understand and affirm the other is love wearing its everyday clothes. Such love is the stuff of which daily miracles are made.

Kitchen Table Counseling

Maybe you've had an experience something like this: you're having a cup of coffee with a friend who seems rather preoccupied and who, in the course of the conversation says, "You know, some days it's hard to even get out of bed." Or a friend at work you've known for a long time in an almost casual way says, "I think I'm about ready for a week-long binge." Or your cousin who lost a son in a car accident months ago seems strangely "out of it," and tells you that ever since her son's death she just hasn't been able to pull herself together.

It may be that all of these people are asking for help and they've chosen you to share their problems with. So what do you do? What should you say? Should you even *try* to help? It's tough for anyone one to admit to a problem, because many of us grew up to believe that we ought always to be strong and able to handle our own issues. We tend to hide our troubles from other people out of embarrassment, and we likewise may be embarrassed to hear about the problems of others. We may be afraid to fail our friend, or to get in over our heads and not know what to do. We're leery of practicing psychology without a license. But we need to remember what the actress Melina Mercouri once said: "In Greece, we are too poor to have psychiatrists. And so we have friends instead."

So assuming that we do care and want to help, what are we to do? When someone comes to us with a problem, there's no reason to think that we are called upon to solve it. Oftentimes, the worst thing we can do is to offer our solution, let alone tell the story of a similar problem we've heard about. And we certainly aren't called to point out silver linings on other people's dark clouds. The most important thing, once again, is simply to listen. Listening gives our friends a

> Our listening helps reassure others that they're not crazy.

chance to hear themselves speak, and thereby get a sense of perspective. By listening, we show others that we can accept them with their problems as worthy human beings, and that we care about them enough to listen; that in itself means a great deal. By listening, without being upset, embarrassed, excited—a "less anxious presence"—we reassure others that they're not crazy. They get a fresh sense of perspective that's often lost when a problem is endlessly thought about alone.

An unknown author has captured the need for this kind of "kitchen table counseling" (or "water cooler counseling") in a poem called *Please Listen to Me*:

When I ask you to listen to me
and you start giving me advice,
you have not done what I asked.

When I ask you to listen to me
and you begin to tell me why I
shouldn't feel that way
you are telling me
to deny my feelings.

When I ask you to listen to me
and you feel you have to do
something to solve my problems,
you have failed me,
(strange as that may seem).

Listen.

All I ask is that you listen.

Not talk or do
—just hear me.
The giving of advice
can never take the place
of the giving of yourself.

I'm not helpless, or hopeless!

When you do something for me
that I need to do for myself
you contribute to my fear
...and weakness.

But when you accept
the simple fact that
I do feel what I feel
(no matter how irrational
that may seem to you),
then I quit trying to convince you
and can get on with
trying to understand
what's behind my feelings.

And when that's clear,
the answers are obvious.
And you know what?
Your listening made that possible.

Speaking Your Truth

We've been emphasizing listening as a way of showing respect for and acceptance of others, a practical way of fulfilling the Judeo-Christian call to "love your neighbor as yourself." By now you may be wondering, "But what about *my* point of view? When do I get to express what *I* think? And what about the danger of being so open to everything and everyone that I stand up for nothing?" Good questions.

Speaking our truth is a matter of timing. Often, we're so eager to "get our oar in" that we cut in before we really understand where the other is coming from. So, the advice still stands: first of all, listen so carefully as to be able to summarize back to another what she said so clearly that she can say, "Yes, that's exactly what I meant." Second, say out loud what you can agree with, even if it's only, "I also am concerned about...." Only after that is the time ripe to say, "My point of view is..." and, "Here's how I came to this opinion." No, not everyone will be willing even then to listen to your viewpoint, but most people will. You've paid attention to them; most will now be willing to pay attention to you. Probably, neither of you will change your minds. But you'll at least be real people to each other rather than stereotypes, and will have enough in common to stay in relationship. Instead of walking on eggshells around each other, carefully calculating what subjects must be avoided, you'll have moved towards accepting differences as enriching—rather than threatening—life together. That willingness to "hang in there" with one another (rather than perpetual warm, fuzzy feelings) is what love really means.

And let's be clear: openness to other people doesn't mean falling for anything and everything. Reinhold Niebuhr reminded us that Jesus said we should be "wise as serpents and simple as doves;" we have too often, he said, obeyed only the latter half of that advice. Loving our neighbor does not mean letting the neighbor walk all over us, and it certainly doesn't mean accepting behavior that offends against the humanity of others. A true acceptance of others has no room for mere sentimentality—if we value persons, we must reject anything that violates or harms or diminishes persons. There is room in love for anger—anger at any physical, emotional, or intellectual violence that stunts the growth or saps the joy of fellow human beings. In an authentically spiritual person, however, the anger is empty of self-righteousness, since we're well-acquainted with our own faults and foibles. And beyond our anger we are ready to resume the broken relationship once the destructive behavior has been admitted and amended.

That Awful "Institutional Church"

Nowadays, it is commonplace to hear people say, "I consider myself a spiritual person, but I don't want anything to do with the institutional church." (For "institutional church" you may substitute any other regularly gathered religious body.) That reluctance to be identified with the church is understandable, since many have been disillusioned by earlier experiences. They may have been frightened as children by talk of hell, discouraged from questioning, rebelling against fundamentalist intolerance or what a disillusioned former Presbyterian elder called "Neanderthal theology."

John Gardner, the founder of Common Cause, once said that the problem with our political life is that we have unloving critics and uncritical lovers, whereas what we need are loving critics and critical lovers. That's true not only about our political institutions, but educational, social, economic or religious institutions as well. The church—or synagogue, temple, or mosque—also needs loving critics and critical lovers. Simply dismissing religious institutions out of hand makes no more sense than looking at them through rose-colored glasses. In our time, unlike the cultural past, belonging to a religious group is a choice, not an expectation. You may choose not to identify with a religious community, but hopefully you're open to the possibility that it might be a help rather than a hindrance on the road to mature spirituality.

One of the mistakes that currently popular debunkers of Christianity make is the supposition that church people spend all their time arguing about proofs for the existence of God or trying to believe "six impossible things before breakfast." The reality is that churches are often *communities* where individuals are able to break through loneliness and nourish relationships. As Paul the Apostle once advised, "Rejoice with those who rejoice and weep with those who weep." That happens in religious institutions; in small, face-to-face groups, people learn to trust and care for one another. In our increasingly specialized society, where those in one field of work cannot even understand the language of another, church is a place where we may meet simply as human beings. As one university professor of sociology put it, "I show up Sunday after Sunday simply to recover my humanity." Many churches, in their hour of worship, have a period of "joys and concerns," where people speak about what is going on in their lives and ask for support. The prayers that they offer for one another are not a kind of primitive magic, but rather what has been called "the most ancient form of Christian friendship."

Often, we need not so much to hear and learn a new thing as to be reminded of what we already know. And the time of worship reminds us of what life is like when we are most fully alive. It is not that there is one sacred place or time; rather, this place and time is a reminder of the sacredness of all places and of all time. Worship does not mean groveling before an "Almighty King," but acknowledging our nature as dependent and needy beings, not self-sufficient, persons who are connected with the whole creation and with the One "in whom we live and move and have our being." We recall our proper place in the scheme of things, renew our sense of perspective. We wrestle with some of life's big questions, face up to where we fall short of what love and justice require of us, and stir up the ashes of our hope for a better life. In worship, to be brief, we hold up before ourselves a vision of truly humane life, and measure ourselves against it. Where else in our society does that happen with regularity?

Sometimes critics of religion disparage "dry ritual." Heaven knows, ritual may be dry and boring. But not necessarily. Think how, in our personal and family life, ritual is often the spice of life. Perhaps Christmas must always be celebrated in exactly the same way, with milk and cookies left for Santa. Think about the lanky, moody eighth-grader, hormones just kicking in, who still hopes still to be tucked in by his mom at bedtime. Think of the old couple who daily hold hands over a glass of wine at "Happy Hour." Our lives are often enriched and measured by their rituals. Whether or not it takes a village to raise a child, the religious community does recognize and celebrate the significant occasions of life: an infant *oohed* and *aahed* over at baptism, an adolescent invited to adult privileges and responsibilities at confirmation, a couple's union blessed at wedding, a life remembered at time of death. Ritual religious acts are a way of symbolizing, rather than just talking about, life's meanings. And especially at crisis times, when our individual capacity for originality is at low ebb, we need these dependable rituals that remind us who we are and keep us from being alone.

Institutions—political, social, educational, as well as religious—inevitably disappoint us. But it makes little sense to wash our hands of them and stand apart in splendid isolation, as though we do not ourselves share in their imperfection. The plain fact is that we need to link arms with others to accomplish much of anything in this world, and that's as true of religion as anything else. Any good idea has to be *incarnated*—take tangible form—if it is to have any influence over time. And the name for that tangible linkage of persons, spiritually speaking, is *institutional religion.*

So let's suppose that you're open to the possibility of becoming part of a religious community. What should you look for?

It doesn't really matter whether the community meets in a theater or a Gothic cathedral, whether the officiant wears a clerical robe or blue jeans, whether the instrument of praise is an organ or guitar. Look for a community that:

- *not only tolerates, but encourages doubt and skepticism of inherited tradition*
- *relates ancient wisdom (Scripture) to contemporary issues, giving worship the "odor" of reality*
- *embraces diversity, whether of race, economic standing, sexual orientation, or politics*

- *provides face-to-face groups where people can learn to be ministers to each other*
- *harvests the insights of all, instead of passively accepting the words of preacher, priest, or imam*
- *cultivates a sense of humor, never confusing metaphors of the sacred for the Sacred itself*
- *trusts that it's better to believe too little than too much, and good to rest content with many questions unanswered*
- *and provides a vision of the human future that is at odds with what passes currently for reality.*

Such is the nature of a religious community—well worth searching for—that enables us with intellectual honesty to be part of a group in which our loneliness is swallowed up and our spiritual search enhanced. It is also a community which challenges us to make a difference in the world, to be part of what Judaism calls *tikkun olam*—"repairing the world." To that dimension of the religious life we now turn.

Chapter 4

Our Hunger for a Better World

The hungers of the human heart go beyond struggles for selfhood and for relationship. We also long for a better world.

Who among us does not lament the suffering and evil that mark the human story as tragedy? Unending warfare and uncured diseases, sexual abuse and torture, befouled seas and heartbreaking poverty—the list goes on and on. And who is not tempted just to shut it out, to try to protect ourselves by developing a calloused heart? Yet most of us know that we cannot do so. We are not solitary souls, but citizens of a species and sharers of a planet. We are responsible to live as healthy cells in the body politic. And so we can't escape the question: What do the world's troubles have to do with my spirituality? What is my role in *tikkun olam*—the "repair of the world"?

Rearranging the Furniture

From the Buddhist tradition comes the story of a monk who had been in a monastery for many, many years, who at long last experienced enlightenment. At that moment, he was required to leave the place of security and contemplation.

He had mixed feelings: sadness at leaving and uncertainty about his future, but also excitement because a gift was traditionally given to each departing monk. His monastery was a treasure house of rare scrolls, beautiful artworks, precious jewels, and as he waited in line before the master he saw other monks receive such valuable gifts.

When he reached the head of the line the master asked what he now planned to do. The monk replied that he didn't really know, but would return to his ancestral home. The master nodded and handed him his gift—a box. The monk admired its simple beauty, but was most excited about what it might contain. Yet, when he opened it, to his surprise he found nothing. Hiding his disappointment, he left the monastery and returned to the humble home that had been left to him by his now deceased parents.

Though disappointed with his gift, the monk placed the box in a place of honor—on the mantel in the living room. But when he stepped back to look at it, it didn't seem quite right. And so he began rearranging the other things on the mantel until, after a couple of hours, it finally looked right to him.

He stepped back to admire his work. But with the mantel rearranged, the living room didn't seem quite right. And so he began again moving things—the small tables, the few screens and pillows—until he was satisfied with the room's appearance. Now, being hungry, he went into the kitchen, but the kitchen didn't feel right. With the mantel and living room rearranged, something was wrong in this room. And so he went to work until, some hours later, he went into his bedroom to rest. But now the bedroom didn't seem right. And so he set to work once more until, many hours later, the room seemed good to him and he fell down exhausted and went to sleep.

When he woke up he decided to take a stroll in the garden, but when he looked out on the garden it happened again. With the mantel, the living room, the kitchen, the bedroom nicely rearranged, the garden had to be redone. This of course took much longer. It took months until, with the bushes dug up and replanted and the paths reset, the feeling of wrongness finally went away. Now at last, his home was complete.

Then one morning he walked out of his garden and into the wider world. At once that old, uncomfortable feeling returned, stronger than ever. Deeply disturbed by what he had gone through since receiving the box, in frustration the monk wrote a letter to his master. He explained that when he had put the box on the mantel, the mantel had not seemed right, and then all because of the box he had to arrange also the living room, the kitchen, the bedroom, and the garden. And now, when he faced the world, what did the master expect? That he should rearrange the whole world?

A few weeks later a reply came from the master. The letter had only one word in it: "Yes." The monk left home and walked out into the world.

Let's admit right away that none of us, all alone, can rearrange the world, can make it right. But that story from the Buddhist tradition also goes straight to the heart of the Judeo-Christian tradition into which most of us have been born. Contrary to the common view that religion is about merely personal belief (nobody else's business), the biblical tradition is above all about our duty in the wider world—about compassion for the poor, about justice in national life, about the common good. It calls us to tether our lives to grand purposes—purposes that go far beyond our own full stomachs, our 48-inch television sets, and our secure 401(k)s. We are called to be part of the healing the hurts of the world, part of *tikkun olam*.

Imagining Another World

On a March 2, 2010 broadcast, the commentator Glenn Beck (himself a Mormon) lashed out at Christian involvement in social causes. "I beg you," he said, "look for the words 'social justice' or 'economic justice' on your church website. If you find it, run as fast as you can. 'Social justice' and 'economic justice,' they are code words. Now, am I advising people to leave their church? Yes."

Well, if "social justice" is a code word for anything, it is for the basic biblical message of what authentic religion requires.

The great Hebrew sages—Amos, Micah, Jeremiah, Isaiah—all spoke of a God who wasn't very interested in religion, but was passionate about justice. They all saw unjust wealth and oppression in their society as an offense against the Sacred. We call them *prophets*, a word which did not refer to predictors of the distant future, but homegrown critics of Israelite society when it failed to meet the criteria of divine justice. And what was their indictment? In no uncertain terms they denounced those who lived in luxury while neglecting the poor, who set up dishonest scales in the marketplace, who withheld wages from

The great Hebrew sages spoke of a God who wasn't very interested in religion.

day laborers, who added house to house and land to land, who disregarded the needs of widows and orphans, who bribed public officials, who subverted the common welfare for personal gain.

At the same time, the prophets poured contempt on religious practices that gave people a false sense of security while their society was coming apart at the seams. For example, the prophet Amos, in the name of God, says:

"I hate, I despise your festivals,
  and I take no delight in your
  solemn assemblies.
Even though you offer me your burnt
   offerings and grain offerings,
  I will not accept them;
and the offerings of well-being of
   your fatted animals,
  I will not look upon.
Take away from me the noise of your
   songs;
I will not listen to the melody of
   your harps.
But let justice roll down like waters,
  and righteousness like an
   ever-flowing stream."

And what is "justice?" At its heart, justice means that all the people of God have enough for the savoring of life, and none too much. A modern ethicist argues that in a just society, the rules would be set without anyone knowing in advance where they would find themselves in that society. In other words, no matter what the circumstances of birth, one's needs would be met as well as anyone else's, and life's opportunities would be as available. Justice is the form that love takes in the less intimate relationships of society. Quite obviously, we have a long way to go before the child born to a Harlem cart pusher (let alone a Congolese villager) has the possibilities for food, shelter, education and the pursuit of happiness available to the child of a Wall Street CEO (or, indeed, the average middle class American.)

When those Hebrew prophets look towards the future, they imagine what the world will look like when the Divine purpose for it is fulfilled. In that future, they say (using images from their own place and time), people will build houses and get to live in them without them being taken by others, each person will dwell in security beneath his own vine and fig tree, children will no longer die in infancy, old people will live out a full lifespan, and "they shall not hurt or destroy in all my holy mountain." The most notable thing about this imagining is that the new world is not Heaven, but is Earth renewed, fulfilling its sacred destiny. True, the vision does include some utopian notes ("the wolf shall lie down with the lamb," which might mean a short lifespan for the lamb), but basically the picture is of Earth no longer defiled by human greed and violence. It is humankind's fulfillment of the Master's *"Yes!"* It is Earth "repaired."

Nor is the vision any different in what Christians call the *New Testament*. Though the book of *Leviticus*, with which Jesus grew up, is full of a variety of cultic, ritual, dietary, and moral laws, from it he quoted only one guideline: "You shall love your neighbor as yourself." His ethic was as profound as it was simple: "Be compassionate, as God is compassionate." The early Church remembered him saying, "I was hungry and you gave me food, I was thirsty and you gave me something to drink, I was a stranger and you welcomed me, I was naked and you gave me clothing, I was sick and you took care of me, I was in prison and you visited me." When (in this parable of Last Judgment) the righteous protest that they don't remember doing all this for him, he answers, "As you did it to one of the least of these, you did it to me."

A Not-Too-Bright Samaritan?

Jesus typically taught by means of pointed, challenging stories that forced people to take a hard look at their own attitudes and behavior. Here's one that I'm sure you remember.

One day, Jesus said, a man was traveling the road from Jerusalem to Jericho when he got mugged, stripped, beat up and left half dead. When some religious types (a "priest" and "Levite"—Temple officials) who were going that way spotted him, they took a quick look, did nothing to help, and kept on walking. Then a Samaritan (member of a looked-down-on minority) came by and was shocked by the poor guy's condition: he washed and dressed his wounds, hoisted him up on the donkey he was riding, took him to a wayside inn and looked after him. The next day he paid the bill for both of them, and asked the innkeeper to take care of the stranger, promising that "when I come back this way, I'll pay you whatever else it has cost for you to care for him." Jesus was obviously challenging his listeners with a question, "Would you act with as much compassion as that guy you look down on?" And ever since we've known that guy as the "Good" Samaritan.

But now let's extend the story a bit. As Jesus told it, the Samaritan promised to reimburse the innkeeper for any additional expense he might incur "when I come back this way." So we're invited to imagine that he took that same route often. Suppose, then, that a week later, as the Samaritan was traveling down the same road, he again came across someone who had been beaten, robbed, and left by the side of the road half dead. What would he do? We might imagine that he would approach that victim also, cleanse and bandage his wounds, take him to the inn, and pay the bill for his lodging and care.

But what if it happened again the following week? And the one after that? What if every time he came that way he found victims of a band of robbers? If he continued to meet all their needs himself, he would certainly be a very *good* Samaritan— but perhaps not a very bright one. Sooner or later it ought to dawn on him that his personal resources weren't adequate to the needs he faced. Surely he would wake up to the realization that instead of bandaging victims week after week, somebody should start patrolling the road so there'd be no more victims. In other words, he would realize that *personal charity is no substitute for social justice.*

Of course, we need both: charity and justice. It's good to take canned goods to a hunger center when this very weekend some families in our town would otherwise go hungry. But it's also important to ask *why* some of our neighbors are hungry—and to change the conditions that allow hunger to persist. Of course, that *why* question gets us into politics and economics. And that's where otherwise good people tend to get skittish.

But "politics" and "economics" are not dirty words. They are about how communities of people organize their common life, allocate their resources, and tackle their shared problems. They're about our *values,* and about how we help one another when our problems are too big for individual acts of charity to solve. And, as we've seen, in the biblical tradition the words *ethics* and *social* belong together. *Knowing God*—in the biblical tradition—has to do not just with warmth in one's heart, but with honesty, fairness and abundance in the common life called "society." And that takes our involvement in the public arena. We live in a time when a single act of Congress or stroke of a presidential pen can either enhance or undo literally millions of individual acts of charity. How can we avoid getting involved in those decisions?

Whether we look at the Jewish Tanakh or the Christian Gospel, we find the same call. The summary by the prophet Micah can stand for the whole of scripture:

> "God has told you, O mortal, what is
> good;
> and what does the Lord require of
> you,
> but to do justice, and to love kindness,
> and to walk humbly with your God?"

Is it unrealistic to hope for and work for a rearranged world in which the furniture is all in its proper place? Is it unrealistic to work towards a world without hunger, without abuse, without ecological catastrophe, without nuclear nightmare, without war and violence? Or is it perhaps true that we human beings are measured by the quality of our dreams, so that the future we imagine is likely to be the future that we get?

Toward a Planetary Patriotism

Perhaps once upon a time it seemed foolishly idealistic to imagine a truly just and peaceable world. But we are a generation that knows it to be an absolute imperative if our species is to have a livable future. We've learned that garbage dumped off the coast of New Jersey ends up polluting the North Sea, that injustice in the Middle East brings terrorism to New York City, that economic policy in China affects Wal-Mart prices in America, that you can't stop AIDS in Chicago without stopping it in Uganda. The planet Earth pays no attention to national boundaries; therefore, outmoded notions of sovereignty must give way to new mechanisms for common security and global well-being.

> Maybe we're measured by the quality of our dreams, and the future we imagine is the one we're likely to get.

No group has seen the imperative for new ways of thinking more clearly than those who have seen the Earth from space. They formed the Association of Space Explorers to alert humanity to what they learned by looking back at our small, blue and green planet floating against the black backdrop of space. One of them, the American astronaut, Russell Schweickart, wrote:

> "You go around it in an hour and a half. You begin to recognize that your identity is with that whole thing, and that makes a change. You look down there and you can't imagine how many borders and boundaries you cross again and again and again, and you don't even see them...hundreds of people killing each other over some imaginary line that you're not even aware of, that you can't see. And from where you see it the thing is a whole and is so beautiful; and you wish you could take one in each hand and say, 'Look! Look at it from this perspective, look at that!'...You look down and you see that surface of that globe that you've lived on all this

time, and you know all those people down there and they are like you, they <u>are</u> you…From where you see it, the thing is a whole and is so beautiful…."

A Saudi Arabian astronaut (did you realize that astronauts from Syria, Saudi Arabia, Germany, Vietnam, Mongolia, Poland, Czechoslovakia, France, Romania, Canada, India, Cuba, Bulgaria, Mexico, Hungary, Vietnam and the Netherlands, as well as the USA and former USSR have been in space?), Sultan bin Salman Al Saud, described looking back at the Earth through a spaceship porthole: "The first day or so, we all pointed to our countries. The third or fourth day, we were pointing to our continents. By the fifth day, we were aware of only one Earth."

Humanity's next great step forward is to cultivate a sense of *planetary patriotism*, in which we understand ourselves to be citizens not of one country alone, but of Earth. Does that mean some utopian withering away of nations? Not at all. As Israel's Golda Meir once observed, globalism does not mean the end of individual nations any more than orchestras mean the end of violins. But is this sense of human unity an impossible dream? Is it utterly unrealistic?

You may recall that after the brutal violence that shattered the Balkans a decade ago, our government's spy satellites and U-2 planes discovered the existence of a mass grave in Bosnia, at the very spot where many hundreds of Muslim boys and men had been rounded up and then "disappeared." Is that the best we can do—verify massacres after they occur, but not stop them before they happen? Clearly, our evolution towards structures of global security has not progressed far enough. But why should we assume that our present system of nation-states is the final step in human social evolution? Once upon a time our species lived simply in small family groups, then in tribes, eventually in city-states, then small fiefdoms, empires and nations. What shall our next step be?

As we look at our present jumble of some 180 national sovereignties, it's instructive to take a glance backward at the American colonies under the Articles of Confederation. They had then just enough sense of common danger to have gotten loosely together, but not enough sense of shared destiny to forge a common future. In those days before the adoption of our Constitution people didn't say, "The United States *is* this or that," but rather, "The United States *are*...." George Washington couldn't get troops from Virginia to pledge loyalty to the new nation because they said, "Virginia is our country." Each state was a little sovereignty: Massachusetts coined its own money; Delaware had its own navy; ships from New Jersey had to clear customs in New York; Philadelphia merchants wouldn't take New Jersey's money; settlers from Connecticut were fired upon when they crossed the border into Pennsylvania. And through the long summer of 1787 it was touch-and-go as to whether those quarreling sovereignties would yield up enough of their sovereignty to "provide for the common defense, promote the general welfare, and secure the blessings of liberty" to themselves and their posterity. That's about where the whole world is today: just enough sense of common threat to have created a United Nations, but not enough commitment to a shared destiny to give it the authority and resources to do its job.

We're often told that politics is the art of the possible. But that's where religion comes in. *The purpose of religion is to extend the boundaries of what is considered possible.* It has been wisely said that "impossible only means that it hasn't happened yet." The world's enduring religious traditions hold before us grander dreams of what the human community can yet become. Martin Luther King, Jr. expressed his hope for the future into a poem entitled *One Day*:

One day,

Youngsters will learn words they will not understand.

Children from India will ask: "What is hunger?"

Children from Alabama will ask: "What is racial segregation?"

Children from Hiroshima will ask: "What is the atomic bomb?"

Children at school will ask: "What is war?"

You will answer them.

You will tell them:

"Those words are not used anymore.

Like stagecoaches, galleys, or slavery.

Words no longer meaningful.

That is why they have been removed from dictionaries.

When that day comes, we will have realized the fulfillment of an ancient, biblical dream. Today, the question each of us faces is, "How can I be part of rearranging the furniture of the world?"

"I've Got Great News!"

Once upon a time (as all good stories go) an army lay in wait outside a forest to encounter the enemy. However, the location of the enemy troops was unknown, and so, under cover of darkness, a scout crept out through the forest to locate them. His buddies kept a vigilant watch all night long, anxiously awaiting his return. At the first crack of dawn, the bedraggled scout stumbled in to the campsite and excitedly proclaimed, "I've got great news! We're surrounded—we can attack *anywhere*!"

Well, anyone who is sensitive to the state of the world will have a feeling that "we're surrounded." But it takes faith to know ourselves surrounded by evil and injustice and still be able to say, "I have great news—we can attack anywhere!" But that's exactly what our religious tradition affirms: that fullness of life comes not from evading the fight, but from becoming involved in the struggle to extend the realm of justice and love in an often violent and always hurting world.

The spiritual life has no room for illusion and sentimentality about the shape the world is in. We are indeed surrounded by sin and evil. And sin (to use another out-of-fashion word) is inescapably social. We see it not only in obvious outrages against human dignity—selling young girls into sexual slavery in Thailand, or shielding pedophile priests in Boston, or slaughtering worshippers in Pakistani mosques. We see it also among those who go to work in Brooks Brothers suits and have a degree of fame in the human community. Obvious violence troubles us, but we are plagued as well by often hidden violence: from pharmaceutical companies who fudge the results of their tests, payday lenders who gouge the poor who live from paycheck to paycheck, police officers who make color-coded traffic stops. And recently we've seen how people of great reputation can behave, wittingly or unwittingly, in ways that are destructive of the common good.

Today our country is still reeling from an economic crisis that has left millions without jobs, or without homes, which have been lost to foreclosure, or whose retirements are in jeopardy as their investments have plummeted in value. How did we get to such a place? One review of a book about the meltdown was titled "Greed Layered on Greed, Frosted with Recklessness." Well, certainly greed and recklessness—along with corporate arrogance and congressional collusion—played their role. And yet something even more basic was at stake.

That something was revealed in testimony before a congressional committee by Alan Greenspan, appointed to his post as chairman of the Federal Reserve by Ronald Reagan and continuing for eighteen years under presidencies both Republican and Democrat. A staunch foe of government regulation, Greenspan put his trust in the wisdom and virtue of Wall Street. But now he acknowledged that his faith had been shaken: "Those of us who have looked to the self-interest of lending institutions to protect shareholders' equity—myself, especially—are in a state of shocked disbelief." He went on to say that the failure of banks to regulate themselves for the sake of the common good was "a flaw in the model that I perceived as the critical functioning structure that defines how the world works." (As one critic commented, "That's a hell of a big thing to find a flaw in.") He was, in other words, shocked to discover that the titans of finance were "sinners"—putting their self-interest ahead of the common good.

Of course, this economic disaster can't be placed at the feet of one man alone. Congress, which for two decades treated Greenspan like the Delphi Oracle bringing messages from the gods, dismantled protective regulations going all the way back to the Great Depression. Rating agencies, on whose integrity investors depended, were asleep at the switch; as one staff member at Standard & Poor's wrote in an email to a colleague, a deal "could be structured by cows and we would rate it." People of wealth and power have persuaded us that our economic system is part of the natural order of things; they called the collapse a "financial tsunami," as though it was a force of nature that no one could either foresee or prevent. But that is a lie and has always been a lie. Human beings create economic policy, and those who manipulate it for their own benefit are always

Authentic religion is always critical of existing institutions, so far as they betray the common good.

eager to baptize it with the holy water of natural law. A cartoon tells the truth: two titans of finance sit in their overstuffed chairs at the Club, and one speaks to the other; "And I say, if there's a 'trickle down,' there must be a leak somewhere!"

So how is this "great news?" Someone has said that we are invited to join the "joyful resistance movement" of Jesus. He recognizes that authentic religion is always counter-cultural, always critical of existing institutions so far as they betray the common good. Joyful resistance means that spiritual persons are willing to take risks, but also know a certain happiness that comes from living not just for self, but for significance.

What does life look like when attacking "anywhere" we are surrounded by social sin? A hunger activist who has worked in Washington, D.C. at the daunting task of trying to make a dent in worldwide poverty offers a clue. When a visitor asked him what keeps him from despair, how he can keep going in the face of such great odds, he answered, "What you have to have is two things. First of all, you have to have a *vision*. And second, you need to be able to celebrate *incremental victories*." Those are both aspects of mature spirituality: a vision that extends the boundaries of what is considered practical and possible, and the patience to celebrate small victories, knowing that despite our best efforts we will all go to our graves in a world that is yet unrepaired.

Beyond Consecrated Ignorance

If we are to be part of repairing the world, it is not enough to cultivate a vision and celebrate small victories. We also need to shed our "lone wolf" style of spirituality and join with others in shared tasks. There are, of course, many worthwhile groups working both for short-term relief of human suffering (charity) and long-term reform of systems that allow or create suffering (justice). Among these are religious communities.

Lately, we've experienced a good deal of controversy about the role of organized religion in civic life. One of the factors bringing atheists out of the closet and into the public arena has been their concern about the influence of the "religious right" on public policy. But there is, in all of this discussion, a good deal of misunderstanding, especially about the meaning of "separation of Church and State." The First Amendment forbids government to put barriers in the way of religious freedom, or to identify itself with any particular religious body. That is, we are to have no state-sponsored church. However, this separation has never meant forbidding advocacy of religious values in the public arena. Missouri Synod Lutherans, let us say, have the same rights as the NRA or AMA in attempting to influence public policy in the direction of their most cherished values. Whether it be a Catholic bishop speaking about abortion, a Southern Baptist TV evangelist inveighing against pornography, or a Unitarian assembly speaking against the war in Iraq, these and all other such groups have a right to enter the dialogue in the public arena. Rather than wring our hands at their influence, those of us with quite different religious viewpoints should work harder to get our own perspectives into the public mix. In fact, any religious community worth its salt will try to plow its deepest values into the soil of public policy.

But there are a number of cautions we are well advised to pay attention to as we enter the public arena, whether as individuals or religious communities.

"Consecrated ignorance is still ignorance." With those sharp words, Reinhold Niebuhr warned us against simplistic answers to complex social questions. So when we choose to speak about public issues, we need to do our homework very carefully, otherwise no one will take us seriously—or should. We also need to choose our issues carefully, not becoming "a centipede with one foot in every cause." We need also to recognize that one cannot draw straight lines from ancient scriptures to contemporary society, and therefore we need distinguish between what we might call the "divine imperative" and pragmatic human judgments. For example, we understand that it is in the purpose of God that we be reconciled to our enemies. But that does not relieve us of the hard work of weighing the relative merits of this or that proposal to control nuclear weapons, for example, or to make peace in Israel/Palestine. And we need to distinguish between the *political* and the *partisan*. We are necessarily involved in the political realm because that's where society's values are expressed and its decisions hammered out. But the church—or the temple, or the mosque— must never be co-opted by any politician, party, or platform. The religious vision transcends all groups and causes, and must not be co-opted by any of them.

Religious groups must always also appeal to commonly shared values rather than "revelation." That is to say, it is not enough to quote verses from the Tanakh or the Gospels or the Qur'an and expect to persuade others in the public arena. Rather, we must translate such values as we have inherited in our traditions into the language and the common values of the wider community.

Finally, when as individuals or churches we participate in the public arena, we need always to remember that, in the words of the prophet Isaiah, "my thoughts are not your thoughts; neither are your ways my ways, says the Lord." To put it bluntly, on any given policy question we might turn out to be dead wrong. Nevertheless, we must take the risk of weighing, deciding, and acting, if our values are not to lie useless behind our front door or stained glass window. There is no safe neutrality to which we can flee when it comes to the difficult questions of our common life. As Bishop Desmond Tutu once reminded us, "If an elephant is standing on the tail of a mouse and you remain neutral, the mouse will not appreciate your neutrality." And so, as we move from the personal concerns of spiritual life into matters of the wider world, as we try to rearrange the furniture of society, we need to do so with eyes wide open and with these cautions always before us.

And finally, we need to recognize that we may make enemies and run risks. The reality is that unjust and violent powers do not easily give up their control in this world. If we begin to act upon the vision of a more compassionate and just world, we will indeed find ourselves in a resistance movement.

Do What You Can

Around the end of the first century, there appeared what may have been the first handbook for the ordering of Christian church life, called the *Didache*, or the *Teaching of the Apostles*. And this little handbook dealt with a challenge that was troubling the early church. There seems to have been conflict between traveling "prophets" who imitated the radical itinerant ministry that marked Jesus' original movement and those who had jobs to attend to, children to raise, meals to cook—who could not or would not abandon all to be fulltime door-to-door evangelists. To such people the writer of the *Didache* offered encouragement: if you cannot take up the full "yoke of Christ," he wrote, then "do what you can."

Do what you can. Not bad advice for those of us who are overwhelmed by what historian Will Durant called the work of newspapers, scooping up all the villainy of five continents for us to enjoy with our morning breakfast. It's no rationalizing of indifference to say, amidst the staggering global challenges with which we are surrounded, "Do what you can." As Mohandas Gandhi once said, "Almost anything you do will be insignificant, but it is very important that you do it." None of us can do everything, but each of us can do something, and what we can do, we must do. The essayist E.B. White once wrote, "I arise in the morning torn between a desire to improve (or save) the world, and a desire to enjoy (or savor) the world. This makes it hard to plan the day." It should be hard for us to plan our days between saving and savoring, repairing the world and celebrating it. Spirituality holds these two aspects of human experience together: nourishing our sense of wonder and doing what we can to heal the world's hurts.

Sometime back, Bonaro Overstreet expressed for our century what the *Didache* did for the First:

You say the little efforts that I make
will do no good.
They never will prevail
to tip the hovering scale
where justice hangs in balance.
I don't believe I ever thought they would.
But I am prejudiced beyond debate
in favor of my right to choose which side
shall feel the stubborn ounces of my weight.

That's really all you and I have during our brief time in this world—a few stubborn ounces. You have a few, I have a few. But as we find allies in many places around the world and put our stubborn ounces together, we may reasonably hope to tip the scales of human history toward a sacred healing purpose. No doubt at the end of our days, the world will still be marked by its corruptions; but it is no small matter to have been among those who imagined a better day, greeted it in advance, and done what we could to make it a reality.

Only the Furniture?

"I urge each one of you," wrote Ralph Ahlberg, "not to reach the end of your life without having championed some great cause, not without having confronted some impossible outrage, totally, expensively if need be, energetically, with guts and nerve, with prayer and risk. That's how positive change happens." And that was surely the counsel of the Buddhist master.

But is it only the furniture of the house that we are to rearrange? What about the occupant?

And so, in tension with the monk's story, consider another old story, told by a rabbi, of a man on his deathbed, speaking to his gathered children. "When I was a young man," he said, "I set out to change the world. When I found that I couldn't change the world, I set out to change my own community. And now that I am an old man, I see that I should have begun with myself."

So who's right—the monk or the rabbi? Is our calling to heal the injustices of the world, or the distortions of our own souls?

Surely the answer is Yes, and Yes. We can neither wait till we're personally whole to begin work on repairing the world, nor allow our involvement in a good cause to excuse us from self-examination. It's all too easy to confuse our own bitterness and resentment with righteous indignation. We can enjoy yelling at others in the name of peace, and neglecting those nearest to us in our pursuit of justice. It is all too easy to succumb to self-righteousness in the name of a holy purpose. It is useless to work for the world's repair unless our spirits are aligned with our goals; in the words of a great twentieth-century peacemaker, A.J. Muste, "There is no way to peace—peace *is the way*." And so the rabbi was as right as the monk; as the song says, "Let there be peace on earth, and let it begin *with me*."

It may seem strange, but the great champions for justice and peace temper their passion for the world's repair with a lively sense of humor. Richard Deats, deeply involved in the world's hot spots through the Fellowship of Reconciliation, penned a book titled *How to Keep Laughing—Even Though You've*

Considered All the Facts. Robert Muller, head of United Nations agencies dealing with most of the planet's accumulated ills, wrote a *World Joke Book.* Mahatma Gandhi said that "if I had no sense of humor, I should long ago have committed suicide." The martyred Archbishop of San Salvador, Oscar Romero, asked a nun to bring him a fresh joke every morning. "Humor," wrote theologian Harvey Cox, "is hope's last weapon." The lives of all these heroes of justice were not trivial. Humor gave them perspective, a certain distance from despair. And above all, laughter kept them from taking themselves too seriously.

> It's all too easy to succumb to self-righteousness in the name of peace and justice.

They not only worked at rearranging society's furniture.

They began with themselves.

Chapter 5

Beyond a Stingy God

Diana Eck, head of the Pluralism Project at Harvard University, tells in her book *Encountering God* of a dialogue with an elderly Hindu whom she met during her years of study in India. "Uncle" asked a question about her Christian faith.

"Is it true," Uncle asked, "as if verifying an outlandish rumor, that Christians believe Jesus was the only *avatara* [incarnation of God]?" Eck says that she recalled in her mind the language with which she had grown up about the saving uniqueness of Christ—language with which she was now uncomfortable, but which she had to admit was the common Christian understanding. She responded, "Yes, most Christians do. Christians say he was unique, the only one." Uncle continued: "But how is it possible to believe that God showed himself only once, to one people, in one part of the world, and so long ago?" Eck concludes her story, "The implications were clear in the expression on Uncle's face: what kind of stingy God would that be?"

Uncle's question needs to be faced squarely by the world's religions. Are we really to believe that there is "one way" to spiritual truth, that one sacred Scripture has "got it right," that all other traditions are deluded?

Rabbi Abraham Joshua Heschel has written that "in the world of economics, science, and technology, cooperation exists and continues to grow. Even political states, though different in culture and competing with one another, maintain diplomatic relations and strive for coexistence. Only religions are not on speaking terms."

As we shall later see, it is no longer quite true that religions are not on speaking terms—a new day of promising dialogue has begun. But the reality remains that we have a heritage of mutual disdain between religions, which have often contributed to the world's suffering rather than its healing. Where they have not directly caused violence, they have often been silent in the face of it, or even baptized it, allowing themselves to be co-opted by political forces with their own agendas. And so the Catholic theologian Hans Kung has warned, "No peace among nations without peace among religions."

We have indeed come to a day where the interrelationships between the world's religions require that they move beyond the exclusive claims they have made against one another, beyond any concept of a "stingy God."

The New Religious America

As these words are being written, our country is caught up in a sometimes fierce controversy over plans to build an Islamic Center two blocks from "Ground Zero" in New York City. One prominent politician has denounced the proposal as "an assertion of Islamist triumphalism" and part of an "Islamist cultural-political offensive designed to undermine and destroy our civilization." The public and media decibel level is in marked contrast to the virtual public silence that greeted a 29-page letter three years ago from 138 prominent Muslim leaders around the world, addressed to Christian leaders, titled "A Common Word Between Us and You," calling for dialogue toward "contributing to meaningful peace around the world." In the words of one of the signers, "Terrorists don't have the right to speak for Islam...." The contrast between the furor over building an Islamic Center and the silence that greeted a

Muslim invitation to dialogue exposes one of the great unfinished tasks of American democracy.

In the United States, which has become the most religiously diverse nation on the planet, Christians and Jews, Buddhists and Hindus, Muslims and atheists, bump up against one another with regularity. It wasn't always so. If back in colonial America you said "religion," you undoubtedly meant Christian religion, and if you said "Christian religion" you were probably referring to the "Big Three"—Congregational, Episcopal, and Presbyterian versions of Christianity. These were the shapers of the new American culture. Fast forward to the 1950s, when sociologist Will Herberg wrote an influential book titled *Protestant, Catholic, Jew*, thus indicating a modest broadening of the religious base—there were now three acceptable forms of American religion. But largely due to a change in immigration laws in 1965, the scene is very different today. Immigration law had discriminated against persons from the Middle East, the Indian subcontinent or elsewhere in Asia (as late as the 1920s the Supreme Court ruled that no Hindu could be an American citizen—though the question before the Court actually concerned a Sikh!) Suddenly America was open to immigrants of Hindu, Buddhist, Muslim and other faiths.

So today, in a typical Midwestern town, the children in a first-grade classroom will be named not only Kim and Heather and Jonathan, but also Tariq and Tabriz, Kung and Rashni, Zariq and Tizri—and their parents and grandparents will bake cookies for the same PTA meetings and sit together alongside the same soccer fields. Think about other religious changes over the past couple of decades. In 1987 the armed forces established their first Buddhist chaplaincy. In 1991 the House of Representatives was, for the first time, opened with prayer by a Muslim. Mosques, temples, and meditation centers spring up in all our major cities, and today in America there are more Muslims than Presbyterians, or Episcopalians, or Congregationalists—those colonial "Big Three." A Buddhist community in Boulder, Colorado applied to join the Council of Churches; at Harvard, seminary students gather beneath the portraits of Divinity School deans to celebrate Buddha's enlightenment day; a mosque has been built at the Norfolk naval base; the end of Ramadan is celebrated each year at the White house; a Texas town has elected a Muslim mayor; a San Jose computer engineer serves as a Zoroastrian priest; Los Angeles is the most diverse Buddhist city in the world; and the best-selling poet in America is a thirteenth century Muslim mystic.

Many of us would celebrate this diversity, which adds new spice to the American stew. But there's a darker side to the story. In Flint, Michigan a Muslim community found punctured car tires and a parking lot littered with spikes. Mosques in South Carolina, Massachusetts, and Minnesota were destroyed by arson—all *before* 9/11. In Kansas City, a side of beef was hung on a Hindu temple door, mocking that faith's vegetarianism. Statues in a Vietnamese temple in Boston were smashed to bits. Images in a Jain temple in Pittsburgh were destroyed, with a message scrawled across the altar: "Leave." The American tradition of separating the State from particular religious bodies, and promising a welcome to all sorts and conditions of people, is facing a backlash. The jury is still out as to whether, in our generation, we will fulfill that promise.

One Way?

The backlash against an increasingly diverse religious America does not of course always take violent forms. But what we may call "exclusivism," with its dismissive views of other religions, has a long history.

Since Christianity is the dominant religious tradition in the U.S., we need to take a brief look at its exclusivist form. For well over a millennium, the Christian church's dominant refrain, encapsulated in the sayings of popes and councils, was that "outside the church there is no salvation."

If that view sounds antique, a mere remnant of an age long gone, consider much more recent Christian voices. An official of the National Association of Evangelicals has said, "We want it understood that Christians, Buddhists, and Muslims are not praying to the same God. Allah is not Jehovah." (That would come as a surprise to some 14 million Christian Arabs, who regularly pray to "Allah," which is simply the Arabic word for "God.") And when President George W. Bush offered his opinion that Christians and Muslims worship the same God, another prominent Evangelical leader insisted that "he is Commander in Chief, not Theologian in Chief" and that when he concludes that Muslims and Christians worship the same God, "he is simply mistaken." Of course, exclusivism is hardly limited to Christianity. A recent *New York Times* article quotes from a Saudi Arabian school textbook: "It is forbidden for a Muslim to be a loyal friend to someone who does not believe in God and his Prophet" and, "Every religion other than Islam is false." Every great world religion has its own open and closed forms, and its own internal struggle to wage with fundamentalism.

So what's wrong with exclusivism? Several things.

First of all, a moment's reflection makes plain that most of us identify with the religion into which we were born. If you were not born into a Christian family, you were at least born into a culture suffused with Christian ideas and values. If you had been born in Riyadh, you would no doubt be working out your spiritual destiny as a Muslim. If you had been born in Delhi, most likely you would be coping with life as a Hindu. Does this then mean that religion is merely a social artifact, without truth or meaning? No, not at all. But it does mean that each religious tradition responds to the Sacred in a way conditioned by its own geography, history, and culture. It means that the spiritual truth we see is determined by where we stand when we look. This awareness need not make us despair of religion, but should move us to humility, since if we had grown up elsewhere we might see the world through quite a different filter. And that awareness should also make us eager to meet people of other faiths not in order to refute them, but rather to ask how *they* see things. Together, we may find deeper truth than any of us could have found alone.

Another problem with exclusivism is that regarding other faiths as "outside the pale" simply does not square with our human experience. We are always tempted, of course, to compare our saints with their scoundrels, our faith's highest aspirations with their most violent deeds. But the reality is that all religions have both a dark side and have nourished lives of compassion, love, and beauty. In the words of one scholar, "Christians meet Buddhists, Jews, Hindus, Muslims, and Native Americans who not only *say* that they have found peace, and happiness, and a sense of oneness with the Divine in their own religions, but who also show in the way they lives their lives that this is very much the case. These are people who are happy, at peace, and committed to loving each other and improving our world—they sure look 'saved.'" And so a Catholic theologian who greatly influenced the Second Vatican Council, Karl Rahner, insisted that the Catholic missionary who goes to India, for example, can't talk to a Hindu about God as a kindergarten teacher might talk to a child about Australia, assuming that the child had never even heard of Australia; rather, the missionary should assume that God has *already* been part of the Hindu's life, and that from him or her the missionary may even have something to learn.

> We're always tempted to compare our saints with their scoundrels.

And we need to look at exclusive claims in their historical context. Consider, for example, claims made for a man of the first century who was called "Son of God," "Divine," "Lord," and "Savior of the World." I am thinking of Jesus, right? Wrong. Before Jesus was born, all of those titles were given to

Caesar Augustus. So you begin to understand what the early Christian community was saying: if you want to know where the Sacred dwells in this world, look at this humble peasant reformer rather than at the mighty Emperor in Rome. God is to be glimpsed, they were saying, not in conquering armies but in nonviolent compassion. In historical context, those titles call us to a counter-cultural lifestyle, not to theological argument.

Finally, what's wrong with exclusivism is that it fails to understand the nature of religious language. Religious language is overwhelmingly symbolic and metaphorical. Think, for example, of the man who says that he's married to "the most wonderful woman in the world." Would you ever say to him, "Oh, come on now, you haven't tried being married to all the other women in the world, have you?" You'd never say that because you know what kind of language he's using: relationship language, gratitude language, love language. The earliest followers of Jesus similarly spoke like that: in the symbolic language of devotion. It is a great mistake to take such *metaphorical* language and turn it into *metaphysical* language, making the historical Jesus into a deity before whom "every knee must bow."

Diana Eck asks the right question: "How is it that positive commitment to what is true for us has been twisted through the centuries into the negative insistence that nothing else in the world could possibly be true?" We who are Christian need to be clear: to say something positive about the Christ is not, at the same time, to say something negative about the Buddha. Or, as a rabbi once said about his tradition, "I believe God chose the Jewish people. But who said God can make only one choice?"

Are All Religions Saying the Same Thing?

The simple answer to that question is "no."

Pluralism—valuing other religions as well as one's own for the wisdom they contain and the lives they bless—does not mean pretending that all religions are basically alike. We who are pluralists do not assume that all religious ideas and behaviors are legitimate, because there is nonsense and evil in religious as well as in secular life. To argue, as many do, that "all religions are saying the same thing" or "we're all going to the same place" makes little sense. When Muslims affirm belief in one All-powerful God while Buddhists have no god at all, or when

Christians hope for a personal existence in heaven while Hindus aspire to end the cycle of rebirth in a state of *nirvana*, we clearly have to do with very different traditions. What pluralists *do* say is that when one probes beneath the stories and hymns, the myths and metaphors of the great religious traditions, one finds at the heart a common core. That shared core may be simply put: reverence for the Mystery in which all life is set, a seeking for personal integrity and decency, an ethic of compassion for others, and a passion to leave the world a bit more just and peaceable than we found it.

An Anglican priest who spent over forty years in Asia, Murray Rogers, summed up his experience in these words: "Being blessed with friends from these 'other' spiritual paths [Hindu, Buddhist, Taoist] I

> To say something positive about the Christ is not to say something negative about the Buddha.

have grown to know that there are no 'other faiths' except in the most external and sociological terms…. I gladly share without fear of disloyalty to Christ their treasures of experience, their perceptions of the Mystery, their ways of breathing the Reality beyond all name and form. 'I' and 'they' have almost disappeared, and in their place is 'we.'" And a mainstream American interpreter of Christianity, Marcus Borg, speaks for many: "I am convinced …that God, the sacred, 'the More,' is known in all of the major religious traditions, not simply in our own. Indeed, if I thought I had to believe that Christianity was the only way, I could not be Christian."

In 1993, one hundred years after the first such global interreligious conference, thousands of leaders from all of the world's great faiths gathered in Chicago for a Parliament of the World's Religions. At the end of their days of dialogue more than 150 of them, representing Muslim, Jewish, Hindu, Buddhist, Christian, Jain, Zoroastrian, Sikh, Baha'i, Indigenous and other bodies issued a "Declaration Toward a Global Ethic." Aware of the urgent needs of the planet—there is no Jewish ozone layer, no Christian rainforest, no Buddhist ocean—and the hunger, poverty and suffering of human beings, they insisted that "the basis for an ethic already exists." They found a common set of core values in the teachings of their faiths:

"We must treat others as we wish others to treat us. We make a commitment to respect life and dignity, individuality and diversity, so that every person is treated humanely, without exception. We must have patience and acceptance. We must be able to forgive, learning from the past, but never allowing ourselves to be enslaved by memories of hate. Opening our hearts to one another, we must sink our narrow differences for the cause of world community, practicing a culture of solidarity and relatedness. We consider humankind our family."

Obviously, we have a long way to go before reaching that religious ideal of a single global humanity. Voices of intolerance and exclusivism seem sometimes to have a monopoly on the media megaphone. Yet, as that Parliament of the World's Religions demonstrates, there is a strong countermove toward recovering a sense of oneness. The aim is not to try to create one global faith—that is impossible—but to value and learn from our diversity.

Perhaps we may think of it like this: the world's great religions are rather like siblings who were separated at birth and adopted into different families. As they grew up in those families they learned different traditions, told different stories, learned separate customs, perhaps even ate different foods and wore different clothing. But now (in this day of global interdependence and rapid communication) those separated siblings have found one another, and as they look into each other's faces, they see the family resemblance.

Religion and Peacemaking

All of us are aware of how often religions have been called upon to bless violence. One need not look back as far as the Crusades or the Inquisition for evidence of toxic religious passions. It is enough to remember the role of religious extremism in our own time, in places as diverse as Ireland and Sri Lanka, Nigeria and Bosnia. Those same religious leaders who gathered in Chicago for the Parliament of the World's Religions, aware of this dark heritage, said, "Time and again we see leaders and members of religions incite aggression, fanaticism, hate, and xenophobia—even inspire and legitimize violent and bloody conquests. Religion is often misused for purely power-political goals, including war. We are filled with disgust."

But there is another side to the story, seldom reported in the media: the key role of religious bodies in defusing conflict and working for justice, from Nicaragua, the Philippines and South Africa to Eastern Europe. Though many are aware of the role of Pope John Paul II in supporting the Solidarity movement in Poland, and through it, playing an important role in the eventual end of the Soviet empire, few are aware of the role of Reformed churches in overthrowing the Ceauşescu regime in Romania or ending the division of Germany.

Consider the latter example. Throughout the period of the officially atheist Communist state in East Germany, the Church (Reformed and Lutheran) supported and sheltered a nascent peace movement. In 1989, this movement came to fulfillment. The pastor of St. Nicholas Lutheran Church in Leipzig had counseled demonstrators to "put down your rocks"—the Church instructed them in the non-violent strategies of Dietrich Bonhoeffer, Mohandas Gandhi, and Martin Luther King, Jr. On the night of October 8, over 70,000 people marched from St. Nicholas Church into the streets of Leipzig, unarmed, carrying lighted candles. Security officials, fully prepared for a violent "Tiananmen Square solution," waited for instructions from Berlin and Moscow. But the orders never came. One month later, the Berlin Wall fell, effectively marking the end of the Soviet empire and the Cold War. The security chief in Leipzig commented, "We planned everything. We were prepared for everything—except for candles and prayers." That's the other side of religion: mobilizing nonviolent power to defuse conflict; there is power in candles and prayers. Some time after these events, the people of Leipzig strung a huge banner across a major street, which simply said, "We thank you, Church." After the revolution, the church helped people sort out the difference between justice and revenge, and in one startling parable of reconciliation, a pastor took the disgraced and ill former leader Erich Honeker into his own home, even though his own children had been denied higher education by the policies of Honeker and his wife, who was Minister of Education.

Whether in Poland, Romania, Germany—or in the Philippines, where Cardinal Sin had a key role in the downfall of the Marcos regime, or in El Salvador where the martyred Archbishop Romero insisted that the army stop its oppression—organized religion has taken risky and courageous stands on behalf of the marginalized and oppressed. Standing for justice/peace is a sure sign of religion that is authentic.

Meeting Atheists on Common Ground

Daniel Maguire, who is a Catholic professor of theology, has a brother who, once a priest, is now an atheist. In an article in *Christian Century* called "Atheists for Jesus?" Maguire talks about attending a "Freedom from Religion" conference at which his brother spoke. Out of that experience of meeting men and women with a deep moral core and concern for the repair of the world, he came to realize that atheism, or secular humanism, should be recognized as one of the world's religions. "We do not all express the experience of the Sacred in the same way," he wrote. "It need not be translated into 'religious language' or even into a belief in God.... Nevertheless, the perception of the Sacred is the pulsing heart of all moral sensibility."

How can atheism or secular humanism (the "nontheistic" community has its own internal argument about terminology) be taken seriously as "religion?" Maguire responds:

> "Religion is born when human consciousness sees the wonder of our being, the smiles of infants, the beauty of the mallard, the gentle budding of the rose, the generous fecundity of the earth, the fire of heroism, the ecstatic promise of intelligence—when it sees all of this and says, 'Wow!' Do not let the informality of the expression undermine the point. This is the birthstone of awe-full respect and reverent gratitude for the mystery that marks our terrestrial genesis. From this primal awe, moral claims are born; from this primal reverence, religion emanates. The moral response names the gift good; the religious response goes on to proclaim it holy. This is the foundational moral and religious experience and the basis of all civilization. This moment of moral and religious

awakening is marked by a sense of giftedness, whether or not we go on to infer a divine Giver."

Maguire is calling for those of us who find religion meaningful to accept as brothers and sisters in the spiritual search those who have no time for "God talk" and who find organized religion boring, but who work for justice and live in hope; they are, he says, "spiritually bonded with us." Paraphrasing an observation of Simone Weil, he adds that "sometimes those denying God are closer to the reality called 'God' than those who use the name without care."

There are, of course, atheists who can't imagine sharing common ground with the religious. We've had a spate of books lately that express only disdain for religion. But a noteworthy contrary example is provided by the eminent scientist E.O. Wilson, himself an atheist, who recently penned a letter to evangelical pastors, seeking their support in the common task of defending and preserving our planet. (In an article in *The Humanist* magazine, he counseled fellow unbelievers "that if you want to enter a discourse with the religious majority and really make them listen to biology and the fact of evolution, you don't say, 'You poor, ignorant fools, you're harming America!'") In his letter to the pastors, Wilson clearly identified himself as a secular humanist and acknowledged the fundamental differences in their worldviews. "Does this difference in worldviews separate us in all things?" he asked. "It does not. You and I and every other human being strive for the same imperatives of security, freedom of choice, personal dignity, and a cause to believe in larger than ourselves." Wilson went on to say that "religion and science are the two most powerful social forces in the world today, including, especially, the United States. If religion and science could be united on the common ground of biological conservation, the problem would soon be solved. If there is any moral precept shared by people of *all* beliefs, it is that we owe ourselves and future generations a beautiful, rich, and healthful environment."

In his article, Wilson went on to talk about breaking bread with evangelical Christians and sharing days of intense discussion; he has been encouraged by their response. Acknowledging that agreement about fundamental beliefs is not the aim of such dialogue, he concludes, "I found it wonderful to form friendships with people that I thought would otherwise stiffen

> Do I have a "stingy God" or a God whose grace goes deeper and broader than I ever imagined?

up when I got close to them." E.O. Wilson, an atheist, models the readiness for dialogue that all of us ought to aspire to—not checking our convictions at the door, but being willing to listen with openness to where others are coming from, for the sake of our common good.

What can the rest of us, the non-famous, do to move our society away from intolerance towards a genuine pluralism and openness? None of us can do everything, but each of us can do something. Perhaps the place to begin is simply by asking ourselves a few questions: Do I have a "stingy God" or a God whose grace goes deeper and broader than I have ever imagined? Could I invite a few friends to join me over coffee to discuss a good book, say, about the faith of Islam? Do I have a Jewish, or Buddhist, or Hindu acquaintance with whom I can talk about what each of us has valued in growing up in her own tradition? Is it perhaps time for my church to take the lead in creating a community interreligious dialogue group? When I read a letter to the editor in my local newspaper about how all Muslims are terrorists, or about how all who do not accept Christ as savior are going to Hell, might I be the one to respond in the name of a compassionate Jesus? Can we cross faith lines to work together on some common human problem: homelessness, or hunger, or the environment, or war? Perhaps working together is the way to get back "on speaking terms."

Making peace among people of differing religious faiths – or none at all—is a crucial building block of a more just and peaceable planet.

Afterword

Remembering Carl Esenwein

As I mentioned in the Introduction, this book represents my collaboration with a friend, Carl Esenwein, who died on November 4, 2006 after a long struggle with cancer. Carl and I had many conversations about the current state of religion in American culture, and at my request he passed on to me before his death boxes full of notes and texts of sermons that he gave at the Unitarian churches he served in Norfolk, Virginia and Bloomington, Illinois over two decades. This book has grown out of my immersion in them. While responsibility for the final form which this book has taken is mine, its outline and major themes reflect, I am confident, Carl's convictions as well as my own about the meaning of religion and the role of the church in today's world.

Carl grew up in the Southwest and, after working in a family outdoor awning business, left his home in Albuquerque in the early sixties to travel to Chicago to prepare himself for ministry at the Meadville Lombard Theological Seminary. He was sensitive to the urgent needs of the world, and believed that the Church had much to offer persons caught up in that time of rapid social change. The year 1963 was a hopeful time, at the beginning of John F. Kennedy's presidency, and to Carl our national flaws seemed serious, but manageable. He expected in seminary, he said, to find a way beyond the "dog-eat-dog ethic of the business world, persuading people to buy what was not needed, and a poverty of relationships, which put things before people."

He came into the ministry at a time of two great social causes that he, as so many others, found himself drawn to. "We called them both 'movements,'" he said, "the civil rights movement and the anti-war movement. Those of us who identified with these causes felt as though we were soldiers of wisdom and justice and humanity, walking arm in arm into the future." As a seminarian he got deeply involved in struggles of the black community in Chicago, and later would preach eloquently about white oppression and black anger and despair. He accepted a Unitarian pastorate in Norfolk, Virginia, at a time when the country was polarizing over the racial crisis and Vietnam War. Cities were burning and society was coming apart at the seams.

In that context, as one of his church members, Will Frank, later remembered,

> "He always made sure that none would be excluded from this church, and that the disaffected and marginalized would have a voice to empower themselves, both in the church and in the community. He made sure that there was room in this church for the voices of angry Blacks seeking justice, women seeking their own path, youth disaffected from their parents seeking a home in an alien world, gays and lesbians seeking to be themselves. We sometimes squirmed under the harsh critique of demanding voices invited in. It was hard to steer the church safely through the rocks and shoals of troubled times. Yet Carl kept the church together and focused on our moral mission to unite and not divide while the country was tearing itself apart."

The time came, however, when those empowering movements lost steam, the anti-war movement because the war was over, and the civil rights movement because black pride and power displaced white emphasis on integration. Of course, American society did not lack for other causes, and Carl continued to speak and work for many of them: the liberation of women, prison reform, gay and lesbian equality, and so on. But underlying all such involvement with social issues was his conviction that the primary work of the church was to increase in the world the love of God and neighbor. Among much else, that meant eliminating the concept *enemy* from the minds and languages of people, developing human community in which all would be cherished and free to grow, and encouraging and celebrating "victories in every life, joys in the beauty of existence, capacity to love and share."

While Carl always read the biblical story in dialogue with the needs of contemporary society, he was clear that the church could never be primarily identified with a set of social programs. "As long as the church is too closely identified with any given social program, it loses its ability to help people deal with the ambivalence that is a part of almost all human concerns." As another theologian put it, without a sense of the Transcendent, the church would become merely "a footnote in a volume of contemporary sociology." Carl came to the conclusion "that all attempts to deal with social problems are largely irrelevant outside of an extension of human caring." And it was that extension of human caring which he saw to be the basic task of the church.

The main purpose of the church, according to Carl, was "person-building." That meant "helping people grow into the fullest possibilities of their humanness"—developing a strong sense of personal identity, defining their own values, becoming more sensitive in interpersonal relationships, and accepting responsibility for their behavior in the world. It is as "people-builder" that he saw himself as a minister.

Carl once admitted in a sermon that he became a minister without liking ministers very much. One suspects that he was put off by what seemed to him like vocational posing, role-playing and pretending to know too much. He acknowledged trying too hard himself to meet others' expectations. He worked hard at being honest, trying "to sort truth from balderdash," he said, "at times recognizing with embarrassment the latter coming from my own lips." The bottom line is that Carl felt "very humble in the face of the demands of the job of ministry." "The best leader," he said, "...is probably the one who can urge people along, with encouragement and understanding, the same path he himself walks. In this I see a task manageable by such an ordinary person as I." He felt that "perhaps the most important quality I bring to my ministry is patience. ...Although I can't yet and may never grasp solutions adequate to the questions I ask, I am motivated by a dream which for me is what the Unitarian church and its ministry is about; liberation of the human spirit and development of the human capacity for love."

All the tasks involved in the routine of ministry—from management chores to counseling, from repairing office equipment to marrying bright-eyed young people, to holding hands of the sick and downtrodden—expressed his core understanding of the church as a community of people who were a spiritual workshop, building each other up in love and usefulness.

As minister to Unitarian congregations, which tend to be filled with persons who are highly educated, critically minded, and often in reaction against their childhood religious upbringing, Carl emphasized that "we belong to the tradition, too." His sermons were well-stocked with biblical texts and allusions; he clearly understood the Judeo-Christian tradition well, and took it seriously but not literally. At the same time, he recognized that many in his congregations (along with increasing numbers in the wider culture) were experiencing a crisis of belief.

Central to this crisis was a need to rethink the idea of God. Our problem, Carl said, is that "if you use the word 'God' you are likely to be misunderstood, and if you don't use it you have no symbol at all" to speak about life's depth and meaning. Carl used the word "God" to think about our existence beyond the physics and chemistry of it, beyond mass and energy. He found existence in its depths to have a personal character, to be, among its other traits, lavish, extravagant, playful, judging, forgiving, bold, and endlessly creative. He would certainly have agreed with Einstein that either everything is a miracle or nothing is, and for him everything was a miracle. "God" was existence itself in its personal character, evoking our response of reverence and wonder.

Carl's faith was not an institutional hand-me-down, but a living experience. "Divinity," he said, "is not the sort of thing that you should have to use any effort to believe; it is a quality of what clearly exists. To fail to recognize this quality would be to miss the joy and fullness of life…to know God is to know the beauty of existence, the glory of friends, and the wonder of all the creatures around us. No word, no definition is adequate to express our reverence, our amazement, our enjoyment, and our delight." At the same time, he refused to turn a blind eye to life's ambiguities, absurdities and evils; nor would he pretend to have answers to all the dilemmas they raise for us. The words that appear beneath his photograph in the front of this book bear repeating: "Life as we know it," Carl said, "is fragmentary. So is truth as we know it. Let us take what truth we can be sure of and use it boldly, for if we don't struggle to believe too much, at least we can be sure of what we cannot escape believing." Carl's way of being in the world—his integrity, his anger at injustice, his humor, his courage—flowed from connectedness to a sacred Mystery in which he put his trust.

Though Carl was a fine scholar, and his sermons are full of careful analyses of the historical roots of both our problems and our beliefs, he had a mystical side to him that went deeper than reason. That spirit was sometimes captured in parts of worship other than preaching, such as these "Opening Words" for one Easter Sunday service: "Easter is not a time for groping through dusty, musty tomes or tombs.... It is a day to fan the ashes of dead hope, a day to banish doubts and seek the slopes where the sun is rising, to revel in the faith which transports us out of ourselves and the dead past into the vast and inviting unknown." He described that unknown future towards which we and all life move as being "not a chore, but an adventure."

I want to close this section with words from another of Carl's sermons: "We think we know where a person is, yet a person has influence which may be working far from the location of his or her body. We can affect people on the other side of the world, which means, in a sense, we are there." It is also true that we can affect people who are separated from us not by space, but by time, separated from us even as death is separated from life. This I am sure of: we who have known and loved Carl will not relegate him to our short-term memory. As long as we live, so will he; and he will continue to inspire, to encourage, and to befriend us.

Appendix

Why Not Talk It Over...

with some of your friends?

If you found yourself "turned on" by some of the thoughts in this book (or turned *off*, for that matter), why not invite some friends over to your place to talk about it?

One of our problems in today's culture is that religion (along with politics) tends to be a taboo subject. Within families, and among friends, we tiptoe around religious differences, afraid of giving offense or losing our cool. On the other hand, many of us are hungry for some honest conversation. And why not? Both personal spirituality and institutional religion are hugely important in American life. Surely we can learn to talk about them with mutual respect and a quest to understand rather than change one another.

So if you're up for it, gather a group together, and consider these *Discussion Starters:*

Introduction

+ On page 5: "For many people in our day, 'spiritual' is a good word, and 'religious' is a bad word." Is that true for you? If so, why? What do you make of the claim that "spirituality is personal religion, and religion is social spirituality?"

Chapter 1 – Our Hunger to Be "At Home" in the Cosmos

+ On page 9: "'God' is simply a three-letter word, and everything depends upon what a person means by it." What are some meanings you hear when others use that word? What do *you* mean by it?

+ Page 13 has a brief description of the Bible as "not handed down from on high, but coalesced over more than a thousand years." In your growing up, what were you taught about the Bible? How has your mind changed over the years?

+ On page 27: According to Carl Sagan, "…in this sense of seeking the deepest interrelations among things that superficially appear to be sundered, the objectives of religion and science, I believe, are identical or very nearly so." In what ways do you find religious and scientific views to be compatible or in conflict?

+ The chapter concludes (pages 36-41) with four stories from different traditions. Which one speaks most meaningfully to you? Why?

Chapter 2 – Our Hunger to Be Real Persons

+ Page 52: What does the author mean by referring to *duty* as an "antique" word? Do you agree or disagree that our culture emphasizes "feeling good, staying free from commitments, and organizing life around ourselves?"

+ Page 56: "We may use cell phones, iPads, email, and Twitter to stay helpfully 'in touch' with others, or we may use them to keep from getting better acquainted with ourselves." What is your experience with the pace of life and modern communications—do they enhance or clutter up your spiritual life?

+ Page 60: What is your personal response to the assertion that "the faith we have is confidence that this life is meaningful and worthwhile, and doesn't require a life beyond this one to validate it?"

Chapter 3 – Our Hunger for Relationship

+ Page 69: Do you think it's true that we need to "come out of hiding" and "drop the pretense of always having it together" if we are to develop good relationships with others? How do we know when to allow ourselves to be vulnerable and when to set appropriate boundaries?

+ Page 72: Can you think of times when you were hurt because you weren't really listened to, or times when you yourself only half-listened to someone who needed your full attention?

+ Page 79: The author writes of "walking on eggshells around each other, carefully calculating what subjects must be avoided." Can you identify any such subjects in your life with family and/or friends? In avoiding such subjects, what are we afraid of?

+ Pages 85-86: If you are part of a religious community, how closely does it resemble what the author believes is "well worth searching for?" What would you add to, or subtract from, his list of what to look for?

Chapter 4 – Our Hunger for a Better World

+ Page 98: How (and why) does the author distinguish between "personal charity" and "social justice?" Can you suggest situations in which each is the more appropriate response?

+ Page 102ff.: What would "planetary patriotism" look like in practice?

+ Pages 111-112: What are some current examples of religious groups speaking and acting in the public arena? Do you think these involvements are appropriate: why or why not?

+ Page 118: The dying man, once a young activist and now an old man, says that "I should have begun with myself." What might it mean to you personally to begin with yourself? How do you balance that with the need to be involved for social change *before* you "get it together?"

Chapter 5 – Beyond a Stingy God

+ Page 128: "If you had been born in Riyadh, you would no doubt be working out your spiritual destiny as a Muslim." What does it mean for religious commitment that we are so heavily influenced by the circumstances of our birth?

+ Page 133: Re-read the sentence beginning, "That shared core may be simply put...." If that's so, why is there so much distrust and hostility between faith groups?

+ Page 138: Were you aware of this story of the power of nonviolent resistance in Germany, of "candles and prayers?" Why do you suppose so little media attention is given to such stories?

+ Page 139ff.: How might "believers" and "atheists" enter into fruitful dialogue with one another? What might they have in common?

If You'd Like to Dig a Little Deeper....

Here are a few suggestions for further reading..."user-friendly" works that deal helpfully with topics touched upon in this book.

Armstrong, Karen, *Islam: A Short History* (Modern Library, 2002)
A succinct and readable introduction to the Islamic story, from the time of Muhammad to the present day. Some of her other books are heavy going, but you may want to take a look at **The Case for God** *(Knopf, 2009).*

Athill, Diana, *Somewhere Towards the End* (Norton & Co., 2009)
A gracious and engaging memoir by a noted British editor, who in old age reflects on both her atheism and her debt to religion.

Borg, Marcus, *The God We Never Knew* (HarperSanFrancisco, 1997)

One of the best books available to help a person think through what "God" means in the contemporary world.

Borg, Marcus, **Meeting Jesus Again for the First Time** (HarperSanFrancisco, 1994)
A best-selling scholar "unpacks" the gospel story in light of his personal search for the historical Jesus.

Comte-Sponville, Andre, **The Little Book of Atheist Spirituality** (Penguin, 2007)
People of faith will find much spiritual food for thought in this gracious book by a noted French philosopher.

Cox, Harvey, **Many Mansions** (Beacon Press, 1988, 1992)
A warm, personal, very readable account of the noted Harvard theologian's encounters with other faiths.

Crossan, John Dominic, and Watts, Richard, **Who Is Jesus?** (Westminster John Knox Press, 1996)
An introduction to the scholarly search for the Jesus of history, with answers to commonly asked questions.

Eck, Diana, *Encountering God* (Beacon Press, 1993)
Eck, director of the Pluralism Project at Harvard, describes how she was deeply affected by Hindu spirituality during her studies in India.

Eck, Diana, *A New Religious America* (HarperSanFrancisco, 2001)
Describes the changing American religious landscape, with special attention to Buddhists, Hindus and Muslims, and implications for interreligious dialogue.

Esposito, John, *Unholy War: Terror in the Name of Islam* (Oxford University Press, 2002)
An eminent scholar of Islamic history and thought, Esposito brilliantly explains the context out of which bin Laden and al-Qaeda come.

Karabell, Zachary, *Peace Be Upon You* (Vintage, 2008)
Fascinating story of how Muslims, Christians and Jews have interacted from the time of Muhammad to that of bin Laden.

Kimball, Charles, ***When Religion Becomes Evil*** (HarperSanFrancisco, 2002)
Analysis of how and why religion often becomes toxic, with examples ranging from the Crusades to al-Qaeda, by author with extensive Middle East experience.

Lalli, Nica, ***Nothing: Something to Believe In*** (Prometheus, 2007)
Delightful memoir of a girl growing up without religion who as an adult affirms her atheism against a fundamentalist in-law's effort to "save" her.

Meyers, Robin, ***Saving Jesus from the Church*** (Harper One, 2009)
The subtitle says it all: "How to Stop Worshiping Christ and Start Following Jesus."

Myers, David, ***A Friendly Letter to Skeptics and Atheists*** (Jossey-Bass, 2008)
A psychologist draws on social science research to make the case for religion as a positive, health-giving force in human life.

Nhat Hanh, Thich, **Living Buddha, Living Christ** (G. P. Putnam's Sons, 1995)

A major interpreter of the Buddhist tradition to Westerners reflects on spiritual similarities between the Buddha and the Christ.

Sagan, Carl, **The Varieties of Scientific Experience** (Penguin, 2006)

Edited by his widow, Ann Druyan, this is Sagan's "personal view of the search for God," and of science as a kind of "informed worship." You may also want to take a look at his **The Demon-Haunted World: Science As a Candle in the Dark** *(Random House, 1995).*

Teasdale & Cairns, Editors, **The Community of Religions** (Continuum, 1999)

Anthology of voices from the 1993 Parliament of the World's Religions, where 7,000 people gathered in Chicago for the first such Parliament in 100 years.

Tobias, Morrison & Gray, Bettina, Editors, *A Parliament of Souls* (KQED Books, 1995)
From a PBS "special" on the Parliament of the World's Religions, this volume includes conversations with 28 spiritual leaders from many faiths.

Toropov & Buckles, Editors, *The Complete Idiot's Guide to the World's Religions* (Alpha Books, 1997)
Written for beginners (not "idiots!"), this book is clear, accurate and positive in its portrayal of our human religious variety.

Williams, Thomas, *Greater Than You Think* (Faith Words, 2008)
A Catholic thinker responds to "new atheist" arguments in a reader-friendly question-and-answer style.

Wolfe, Michael, Ed., *Taking Back Islam* (Rodale, 2002)
A series of brief essays by American Muslims, interpreting mainstream Islamand challenging extremist understandings and actions.

Wolpe, David, ***Why Faith Matters*** (HarperOne, 2008)
A Jewish thinker called "the #1 Pulpit Rabbi in America" in a Newsweek article responds to the "New Atheists" in a conversational, story-telling style.

Notes

Introduction

Page 3 - On Rilke: from *Letters to a Young Poet*, Wikiquote translation.

Page 4 - On "Living the Questions": Part I, Section 7, "Out Into the World: Challenges Facing Progressive Christians," www.livingthequestions.com LLC, 2010.

Chapter 1 – Our Hunger to Be "At Home" in the Cosmos

Page 9 -"One seeker": Dana Jennings, *The New York Times*, March 2, 2008.

Page 10 - The NFL starter was Reggie White of the Green Bay Packers, *U.S. News & World Report*, May 4, 1998.

Page 10 - The "act of God" reference is from *The Chicago Tribune*, May 4, 1998; "if God is going to take me" was reported in *The New York Times*, December 28, 1990; the Member of Congress was Richard Baker (R-LA), in *Mother Jones*, December, 2005; Katrina as God's judgment, in Robert McElvaine, "Weather of Mass Destruction," *Sightings*, September 29, 2005.

Page 14 - On Kaufman: Cited by Kendig B. Culley in *The New Review of Books and Religion*. For Kaufman's views, see his *In Face of Mystery* (Harvard, 1993).

Page 15 - On Alice and the Queen: Lewis Carroll, *Through the Looking Glass*, chapter 5.

Page 16 - Virgin Mary sighting: Jeremy Miles, "God's Graffiti," *Sightings*, April 28, 2005.

Page 16 - Muhammad inscription: *Chicago Tribune*, May 29, 2008.

Page 16 - "Soft focus veneration": Daniel Dennett, *Breaking the Spell* (Penguin, 2006), 283.

Page 17 - On Sagan: this citation unidentified, but on "skeptical scrutiny" see Carl Sagan, *The Demon-Haunted World: Science As a Candle in the Dark* (Random House, 1995), 304. Sagan has also suggested that "science is, at least in part, informed worship," in *The Varieties of Scientific Experience* (Ann Druyan, Ed., Penguin 2006), 31.

Page 17 - On science and reason: Christopher Hitchens, *God is Not Great* (Twelve, 2007), 5.

Page 19 - On Monty Python: *Monty Python's Contractual Obligation Album*, 1980. More than the quoted hymn verses need critiquing. Consider one original verse of *All Things*

Bright and Beautiful: "The rich man in his castle/ The poor man at his gate/ God made them high and lowly/ And ordered their estate."

Page 22 - On Weinberg: George Johnson, "A Free-for-All on Science and Religion," *Skeptical Inquirer*, March/April 2007, 25.

Page 23 - On King and Bonhoeffer: Hitchens, 173, 7.

Page 23 - On Harris: Sam Harris, *The End of Faith* (Norton, 2005), 184, 190, 192.

Page 27 - Sagan on "exhilaration": *The Demon-Haunted World*, 330. On the objectives of science and religion: *The Varieties of Scientific Experience*, 1.

Page 27 -On de Chardin: cited by T.A. Mathias, "The Living God," a speech on November 20, 1968.

Page 29 - On Douglas Adams: Richard Dawkins, *The God Delusion* (Houghton-Mifflin, 2006), 364.

Page 29 - On Brian Kulick: Julie Salamon, *The New York Times*, February 5, 2004.

Page 30 - On Copeland: from Aaron Copland, "What to Think About Music" (1939).

Page 30 - On "a certain way of looking": source unknown.

Page 31 - "God does not die": Dag Hammarskjold, *Markings* (Knopf, 1964), 56.

Page 31 - On Athill: Diana Athill, *Somewhere Towards the End: A Memoir* (Norton, 2008), 45-46.

Page 34 - "From the altar of the past": Jean Jaures, French Socialist, d.1914.

Page 34 - Dennett quote: *Breaking the Spell*, 155.

Page 35 - "In whom we live and move": *Acts* 17:28.

Page 36 - The Jewish story: *Exodus* 33:12-23.

Page 37 - The Christian story: *Matthew* 14:13-21 & 15:32-39; *Mark* 6:32-44 & 8:1-10; *Luke* 9:10-17; *John* 6:1-14.

Page 38 - On anthropology: Farb & Armelagos, *Consuming Passions: the Anthropology of Eating* (Washington Square, 1980).

Page 39 - "Neither Jew nor Greek": *Galatians* 3:28.

Page 40 - The Hindu story: Diana Eck, *Encountering God* (Beacon, 1993), 82.

Page 41 - David Foster Wallace: in *The Guardian*, September 20, 2008.

Chapter 2 – Our Hunger to Be Real Persons

Page 43 - On Buber: *Time* magazine, June 25, 1965.

Page 43 - "God sends sun to shine": *Matthew* 5:44-45.

Page 45 - On Duncan: Doug Thorpe, "A Conversation with David James Duncan," *Image*, Issue 31, 55-69.

Page 48 - On Merton: Thomas Merton, *Conjectures of a Guilty Bystander* (Image, 1968).

Page 49 - Psychiatric Folksong: in Ravi Zacharias, *Can Man Live Without God?* (Thomas Nelson, 2004).

Page 51 - Native American story: As told by the Rev. Richard Harrison in email to author, May 28, 2010.

Page 54 - On Shaw: from *Man and Superman*.

Page 55 - On "discovering who you are": Nicholas Johnson, "Test Pattern for Living," *Saturday Review*, May 29, 1971, 33.

Page 56 - On email statistics: *Newsweek*, July 26, 2010.

Page 57 - On spirituality of the uneventful: Belden Lane, "Dragons of the Ordinary: the Discomfort of Common Grace," *Christian Century*, August 21-28, 1991.

Page 58 - "Consider the lilies": *Luke* 12:22-28.

Page 59 - Words of St. Paul: *1 Corinthians* 15:19, 32.

Page 60 - On Toynbee: the quotation is from Toynbee, et al., *Man's Concern with Death* (McGraw Hill, 1969), 132.

Page 60 - Words of Norman Cousins: In Connie Goldman, Ed., *The Ageless Spirit* (Fairview, 2004), 49.

Page 61 - Commencement address of Steve Jobs, Stanford University, June 14, 2005.

Page 62 - "Don't cry because it's over": Often attributed to Dr. Seuss (Theodore Geisel).

Page 62 - "The root of the matter": Bertrand Russell, *The Impact of Science on Society* (AMS, 1953).

Chapter 3 – Our Hunger for Relationship

Page 65 - On loneliness: from a student group I worked with at Illinois State University.

Page 67 - On loving brother and sister: *1 John* 4:20.

Page 67 - On Lee Atwater: *The New York Times*, March 17, 1990.

Page 68 - Carl Sagan cited in *The Humanist*, January-February, 2008.

Page 70 - On cell phones: Thomas Seagald, "Pay Attention," *Christian Century*, June 15, 2010, 12.

Page 73 - On proverbs: *Proverbs* 17:27 and 20:5.

Page 77 - Poem on listening: author unknown. Cited in *Preparing for Marriage*, (Augsburg Fortress, 1992), 22.

Page 82 - "Rejoice with those who rejoice": *Romans* 12:15.

Chapter 4 – Our Hunger for a Better World

Page 91 - On Glenn Beck: *The Nation*, June 7, 2010.

Page 93 - "I hate, I despise your festivals": *Amos* 5:21-24.

Page 94 - On justice: John Rawls, *A Theory of Justice* (Harvard, 1999).

Page 94 - On "what the world will look like": see, e.g. *Isaiah* 65.

Page 95 - On love of neighbor: *Leviticus* 19:18; *Matthew* 22:37-40.

Page 95 - "Be compassionate": *Luke* 6:36.

Page 95 - "I was hungry": *Matthew* 25:31-40.

Page 96 - On the Samaritan: *Luke* 10:25-37.

Page 99 - "God has told you what is good": *Micah* 6:8.

Page 101 - On Russell Schweickart: Schweickart, "No Frames, No Boundaries," in Katz et al., Eds., *Earth's Answer* (Harper & Row, 1977).

Page 102 - Saudi astronaut: in Kelley, Ed., *The Home Planet* (Addison-Wesley, 1988), 81.

Page 103 - On the colonies, see Catherine Drinker Bowen, *Miracle at Philadelphia* (Atlantic Monthly Press, 1966).

Page 105- King, Jr. Poem: In "Commonwealth Record of Achievement in Human Rights Education," 10, www.teachers.org.uk.

Page 106 - "Great news!"—as told by George Chauncey, formerly of the Washington Office, Presbyterian Church (U.S.A.).

Page 108 - On Greenspan: see *The New York Times*, October 24, 2008 and *The New Yorker*, February 2, 2008.

Page 109 - On Standard & Poor's: Gretchen Morganson, in *The New York Times*, October 26, 2008.

Page 110 - "Joyful resistance": the phrase is John Taylor's, *Enough Is Enough* (SCM Press, 1975), 68.

Page 114 - "My thoughts are not your thoughts": *Isaiah* 55:8-9.

Page 115 - *The Didache*: see J.D. Crossan, *The Birth of Christianity* (HarperSanFrancisco, 1998), chapter 21.

Page 116 - Will Durant citation: from his "Is Progress a Delusion?" in *Harper's Magazine*, October, 1926, 555-565.

Page 116 - E.B. White: cited in *Newsweek*, October 14, 1985.

Page 117 - Overstreet poem: "Stubborn Ounces," subtitled "To One Who Doubts the Worth of Doing Anything If You Can't Do Everything."

Page 118 - Dying man: my brief paraphrase of Paul F. Cohen, "Elul: A Time for Reflection," *Temple Jeremiah Covenant*, September, 2004.

Chapter 5 – Beyond a Stingy God

Page 122 - Story of Uncle: Eck, *Encountering God*, 82 and Heschel quote, 213.

Page 122 - Words of Hans Kung: Paul Knitter, *Introducing Theologies of Religions* (Orbis, 2002), 102.

Page 123 - Islamic Center controversy: the politician is Newt Gingrich, see *The New Yorker*, August 23, 2010, 27.

Page 123 - Letter from Muslim leaders: *The New York Times*, October 12, 2007.

Page 124 - Supreme Court decision: Eck, *Encountering God*, 36.

Page 125 - Children's names: thanks to Garrett Scott, Oakland Elementary School, Bloomington, IL.

Page 125 - On religious changes in U.S., see Diana Eck, *A New Religious America* (HarperSanFrancisco, 2001).

Page 127 - Evangelical leaders: Richard Cizik, Vice President, National Association of Evangelicals, in *U.S. News & World Report*, May 6, 2002; and Richard Land, President, Southern Baptist Convention, in "World Net Daily," October 7, 2007.

Page 128 - On Saudi textbooks: *The New York Times*, May 24, 2006.

Page 129 - "Christians meet Buddhists": Knitter, 59-60. On Karl Rahner: Knitter, 72.

Page 130 - On first century divine titles, see, e.g., J.D. Crossan, *God and Empire* (Harper One, 2007).

Page 132 - "How is it possible": Eck, *Encountering God*, 96.

Page 132 - On God's choice: Rabbi Michael Kogan.

Page 133 - On Murray Rogers: Eck, 162.

Page 135 - Common core values: in Morgan & Braybrooke, Eds., *Testing the Global Ethic* (CoNexus, 1998), 5.

Page 136 - "Time and again we see leaders": "Towards a Global Ethic," 1993 Parliament of the World's Religions, 3.

Page 137 - "Another side to the story": see Johnston & Samson, Eds., *Religion, the Missing Dimension of Statecraft* (Oxford, 1994).

Page 139 - "Atheists for Jesus?": *Christian Century*, December 8, 1993.

Page 141 - On E.O. Wilson: *The Humanist*, November/December, 2007.

Afterword

Page 149 - On "footnote in a volume of contemporary sociology": I believe the phrase comes from Langdon Gilkey; it is certainly the theme of his book, *How the Church Can Minister to the World Without Losing Itself* (Harper & Row, 1964).

Acknowledgments

I have in earlier pages expressed my gratitude for Carl's friendship and wisdom. I want now to express my thanks to those who have kindly shared their responses to these pages, or in other ways offered their support: Willemina Esenwein, Carl's wife; Marie Genrich, Mark Genrich, Peter Henderson, Lora Oyer, Russell Oyer, M.D., the Rev. James Pruyne and Mary Beth Taylor. Thanks also to Willem Knibbe for the photo of his stepfather found at the beginning of the book.

I owe special thanks to Sehar Azad, whose transcribing skills relieved me of many hours of two-finger word processing, and whose computer savvy saved this technophobe from much frustration. And all that with grace and cheerfulness.

Finally, I'm grateful for the chance to say thanks in this public way to my wife, Charline, with whom I've shared the journey for over fifty-four years, and from whom, together with the Hebrew prophets, I have learned most of what I know about the call to do justice.

As I bring these pages to a close, I feel a deep connectedness with family and friends, teachers, colleagues and congregations, those still among us and those gone from sight. We're all in this together.

Grateful to the One in whom we live and move and have our being, I look forward to the day that is coming, when a just and peaceable planet is full of the knowledge of God, as waters cover the sea.

CPSIA information can be obtained at www.ICGtesting.com
Printed in the USA
LVOW081620190213

320796LV00002B/233/P